Cross-stitch
Garden Projects

Cross-stitch
Garden Projects

Joanne Sanderson

GUILD OF MASTER CRAFTSMAN PUBLICATIONS

First published 2004 by
Guild of Master Craftsman Publications Ltd
Castle Place, 166 High Street,
Lewes, East Sussex BN7 IXU

ISBN I 86108 308 4

A catalogue record for this book is available from the British Library.

Publisher: Paul Richardson
Art Director: Ian Smith
Managing Editor: Gerrie Purcell
Commissioning Editor: April McCroskie
Production Manager: Stuart Poole
Editor: Olivia Underhill
Designers: Phil and Traci Morash at Fineline Studios
Photographer: Christine Richardson
Illustrator: John Yates

Set in Centaur

Colour origination by CTT Reproduction, London
Printed and bound by Kyodo Printing, Singapore

For Alan and Rianna

A special thank you as always to my family for their understanding while I spent many more hours writing and stitching the designs for this, my second book. Especially to my daughter Rianna, who is a constant source of inspiration, and to Alan for his love, support and encouragement.

Thank you to my Mother for all her support and love – you have always given me so much, and to my brother Steven – your encouragement means more to me than you could know.

Thank you to the Lord for all his blessings and Grace.

Acknowledgements

Thank you to the following for helping in making this book possible:

Cara Ackerman at DMC for all the threads and fabrics used in this book, and all my other projects too, always sent without delay.

All the suppliers who kindly sent the products used in finishing and framing the designs.

Thank you to Barbara for helping with the stitching of some of the projects.

Contents

Appendix

Introduction

My love for nature and gardening has given me the inspiration for this, my second book, *Cross-stitch Garden Projects*. I have included a selection of my favourite flowers, along with popular fruit and vegetables — many of which can be completed in only a few hours.

There are plenty of different designs for you to stitch, from simple, small motifs to larger pictures and samplers, both modern and traditional in style. With over 60 charts included, some containing multiple motifs, there is something to suit everyone's taste and skill level. I have included a few other interesting techniques, such as stitching with beads. If you haven't tried this before then have a go — it will take your stitching to a new dimension.

Don't feel you have to follow my suggestions, for example the fruit wall-hanging on pages 112–117 could be stitched as four separate pictures. Many of the motifs can be used in a variety of ways, from adorning clothes and items using waste canvas, to presenting them in small cards, and other gifts.

If you wish to mount your finished designs, I have given instructions as to how to do so, but you could experiment with other ways of finishing your work. I have chosen to use very simple ways of displaying the finished stitching — ready

made frames and bought items that require very little sewing. This is to inspire people who want to have a go but are often put off by complex finishing techniques; for example the clematis cushion on page 136 makes use of a bought cushion cover rather than making one up from scratch. If you wish to make your own cushion then of course you can do so instead.

A stitched gift is always well received and the effort taken is always worth the time spent making them. I always send a stitched card on a loved one's birthday – I usually omit any text on the front and then the card can be framed afterwards as a small picture and reminder of the celebration. Try stitching some of the traditional or contemporary cards; you could use any of the motifs too – just check that the finished design will fit inside a card aperture.

I hope that you will find this book a good source of inspiration and that you will receive as much pleasure out of stitching the items as I have in designing them for you. I always test stitch my own designs and they are designed in such a way as to make them as easy as possible to stitch while still remaining interesting and pretty. I hope this encourages you to stitch the designs you feel inspired to, without having to worry about their difficulty and how many thread changes or colours there are.

Essentials

Materials and Equipment

You only need basic items of material and equipment, much of which is personal preference, to produce the cross-stitch designs included in this book. Below is a list of the most popular items used by stitchers.

Hoops and frames

Whether you use a hoop or scroll frame is down to personal preference, but either will keep the fabric taut and therefore help you to achieve even-tensioned, neat stitches. By mounting the hoop or scroll frame in a stand you have two hands free. I always use a stand when stitching with a hoop as I can stitch much faster. For small projects it may be preferable to simply hold the fabric in your hand while you stitch. A good tip is to spray the fabric you are using with ironing starch and press the fabric to remove the creases. This activates the starch so that the fabric is nice and stiff. If using a frame or hoop, ensure it is big enough to cover the whole design when stitched, and always remove your work from the hoop when not stitching, as this will help prevent nasty, stubborn creases from forming.

Fabric

There are two main types of fabric used in cross stitch – the main one is Aida 14-count. This has 14 x 14 holes per inch (2.5cm), or HPI, and is the most widely used fabric. The stitches are made across one block of fabric. The other type of fabric

is evenweave, for example linen. Stitches are made across two of the strands of thread, the most common type used is 28-count which, when worked over two threads, gives the same-sized stitches and appearance as 14-count Aida. The designs used in this book are stitched mainly on these two fabrics, so either could be used for each project depending on personal preference. Beginners may find it easier to stitch on Aida first and experiment with other fabrics later on.

To work out the size of a finished design, as a rough guide, the higher the HPI the smaller the design will be. For example, a design stitched on

18-count Aida will be smaller than a design stitched on 14-count Aida. Divide the stitch count by the fabric count (holes per inch). For example, to find out how large a design 28 x 42 stitches would be on 14-count fabric, divide 28 by 14, which equals 2, and 42 by 14, which equals 3. The finished design would be 2 x 3in (5.1 x 7.6cm). When working out how much fabric to use, always remember to allow for framing – an excess of fabric of at least 2in (5.1cm) on each of the four sides.

Thread

The designs in this book were stitched using DMC six-stranded cotton thread, which comes in eight-metre skeins. In the United States it is usually referred to as 'floss'. Cut the thread to workable lengths, but no longer than 18in (45.7cm) or they will tangle and knot during stitching. Separate all six strands and recombine

the number stated in the key – two strands is usually enough to give a reasonable coverage with 14-count fabric. For backstitch, one strand is appropriate to achieve a subtle outline. As you work, let go of the needle from time to time and allow the thread to drop down and unravel itself, this will help prevent knots forming. If a knot forms, insert the needle into the knot, work the knot loose and gently pull the thread.

Thread sorter

This is a piece of card with holes punched down the side. I recommend using one for each large project, especially where there are several similar colours. Loop each colour onto the card, remembering to write down the thread number and symbol from the key alongside it. I always make my own from scraps of card but you can buy them from most craft stores.

Needles

Stitch the designs with blunt-ended tapestry needles as these are designed to go through the holes in the fabric easily without piercing or distorting the fabric. I recommend a size 26 or 24 for most of the designs stitched in this book; 26 is smaller – which I prefer – though you may choose size 24 as it really is personal preference. You can buy gold-plated needles which last a lot longer than ordinary nickel-plated ones. They cost a little more, but are a joy to use and are ideal for people who have nickel allergies. Never leave needles in the fabric when not stitching – over a period of time they may mark the fabric.

Scissors

You need a pair of small, sharp embroidery scissors for snipping threads and a pair of dressmakers' scissors for cutting fabric. Never use these scissors for cutting anything else, such as paper, as this will blunt the blades.

Basic Techniques

This section outlines the basic techniques you need to complete the projects listed in this book.

Preparation

Before you begin, note that each square on the chart represents a block of fabric or stitch; the solid lines are backstitch. Each symbol represents a cross stitch. The thread colour is shown in the key. French knots and beads are also indicated.

Method

1. Start in the centre of the design and work outwards unless otherwise stated. To find the centre of the fabric, fold the fabric in half and then in half again, then unfold to reveal the centre where the lines intersect. The centre of the chart can be found by aligning the two arrows. The point where the rows meet is the centre point.

2. Identify each colour with the symbol in the key. I recommend that you use a thread sorter (see Materials and Equipment, page 12) and write the symbol for each colour at the side of the relevant thread along with the DMC reference number as some shades of thread are very similar. Each length of thread is made up of six strands, which you must separate before stitching. Recombine the number of threads in the chosen colour as stated in the key.

3. Start by one of the following two methods:

   a) The waste knot method
   Tie a knot at one end of the thread, push the needle through the front of the fabric to the back a few stitches away from where you need to start, leaving the knot on the front. Stitch towards the knot and, once you reach it and the stitches are secure, snip the knot off. This method is best used for stitching with an odd number of threads, for example when cross stitch in one strand is needed.

   b) The loop method
   Fold one strand of thread in half, thread the two ends together through the needle. Bring the needle up through the fabric from back to front and then through to the back of the fabric to make the first diagonal part of the cross stitch. Pass the needle through the loop and pull the thread tight. This will secure the thread and the stitch can be completed. This method is used when an even number of threads, such as two, is required.

4. To finish, push the needle through to the back of the fabric and weave the thread through several stitches before snipping off neatly, as close to the fabric as possible. Never start or finish with a knot at the back of the work as this can show through to the front. Don't be too concerned with the neatness of the back of the work when stitching, as this can make stitching more of a chore than an enjoyment.

5. Work all cross stitches before completing any backstitch, French knots or beads and charms.

6. Always use an even tension, preferably with the aid of a frame or hoop.

7. All top crosses should lie in the same direction. Do not carry long threads across the back from one area to another as this will affect the tension and might show. Do not use knots as they have a nasty habit of working their way to the front of the fabric.

8. Always make sure that your hands are clean, and keep work in a plastic bag when not stitching so that it remains blemish-free. Do not leave needles in the fabric when not stitching, especially nickel-plated ones — with time these can rust and stain the fabric.

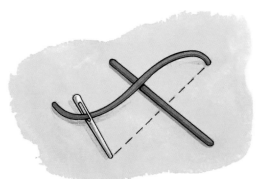

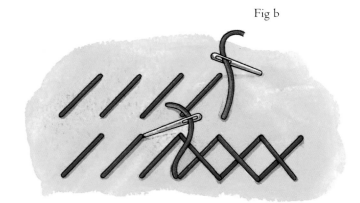

Stitch techniques

Cross stitch

Cross stitches are the main stitch used in this book. They are indicated on the chart by a symbol, each one representing a single cross stitch in the colour indicated by the key at the side of the chart. Unless otherwise stated, always start a design at the centre of the fabric corresponding to the centre of the chart, and work outwards. A cross stitch is worked in two stages over one block of Aida fabric, or over two threads of evenweave fabric. A diagonal stitch is worked first and then a diagonal stitch in the opposite direction to form a cross (Fig a).

It doesn't matter which way you start the diagonal, i.e. from bottom left to top right or bottom right to top left, but it is important to stick to either one so that all top diagonals lie in the same direction to produce a neat, professional finish. I recommend that you complete each stitch as you go along, but for larger areas you may prefer to work in rows. Complete a row of diagonals (the first half of the stitch) and then return along the row stitching the second part of the stitch, the diagonal in the opposite direction (Fig b). When using evenweave fabric, make the stitch over two threads of fabric. When using Aida, make the stitches over one block of fabric.

Three-quarter cross stitch

This is used to achieve a smoother outline to a design, and is shown on the chart where a symbol occupies half of a square. To work a three-quarter stitch, work the first half of the cross stitch, i.e. the first diagonal line, but instead of completing the second diagonal, bring the needle up as usual in the opposite corner but then bring it down in the centre (Fig c). The direction in which the

Fig c

Fig d

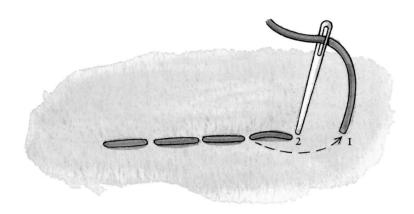

stitch lies is indicated by where the symbol is placed on the chart. If two symbols occupy the same box on the chart, then two of these stitches are completed in the threads indicated by the key. Work the first three-quarter stitch, then using the second colour, complete the stitch to make a whole cross stitch (Fig c).

Half cross stitch

This is a diagonal line usually lying the same way as the top diagonal line that forms the second part of the cross stitch. For example, if your cross stitch consists of a diagonal bottom left to top right with the second part of the top diagonal lying from bottom right to top left, then any half cross stitches are completed bottom right to top left.

Backstitch

This is indicated by a solid line on the chart and is worked usually in one strand of thread. Bring the needle up through the fabric at 1 and down at 2 producing short running-type stitches. Again, when working on evenweave fabric, make the backstitches over two threads of fabric, and with Aida over one block. Backstitch usually follows the cross stitches, but in some cases the lines on the chart do not – these are long stitches, which are worked in exactly the same way as backstitch but each stitch is usually longer in length than one stitch (Fig d).

French knots

These are used on a few of the designs. Bring the needle up through the fabric as shown, hold the fabric taut and wind it around the needle twice. Push the needle back through the fabric slightly to the side of where you brought it up. While continuing to hold the thread taut, take the needle all the way through the back of the fabric. As the thread wraps around the needle, a knot is formed (Fig e). A clever alternative to making a French knot is to replace the stitch with seed beads of the same colour.

Fig e

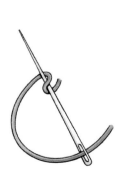

Fig f

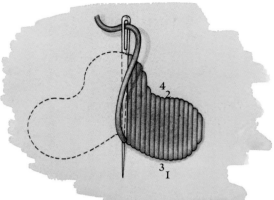

Fig g

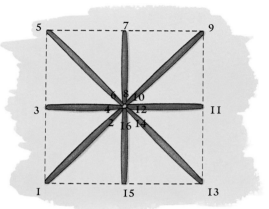

Satin stitch

This is a long stitch that smoothly covers the fabric, as the stitches are worked side by side. Come up at 1, down at 2, up at 3 and down at 4. Always come up and go down on the same side this will mean the back of the fabric will look like the front. Avoid pulling the thread too tight, aim for an even tension to achieve a smooth finish (Fig f).

Algerian eyes

Star-shaped stitches, occupying a square shape. Come up at 1 and down at 2, and so on, working clockwise. Always pass the needle down through the centre and pull firmly. This produces a small 'hole' in the centre, characteristic of this stitch (Fig g).

Ribbon roses

Start by making an odd number of spokes with thread – five is ideal (i). Come up through the centre of the spokes with the threaded ribbon, and weave the ribbon under the first spoke, over the second, under the third and over the fourth. Continue to weave the ribbon until all the thread has been covered (ii). Take the ribbon back through the fabric where you have finished and secure with a few discreet stitches of thread (Fig h).

Fig h

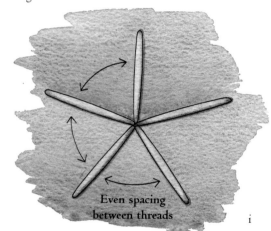

Even spacing between threads

i

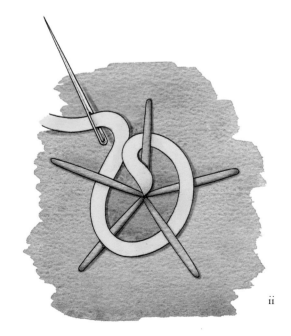

ii

Order of stitching

All designs, unless otherwise stated, should be completed in the following order:

1 Cross stitches
2 Backstitches
3 French knots, beads and charms are added last

Double check that all stitches have been completed before the design is mounted.

Finishing

To finish, the embroidery can be washed and ironed. Follow the manufacturer's instructions provided with the threads and fabric used. Use warm water and a mild detergent. If the colours bleed, keep rinsing under warm water until the water runs clear. Dry the fabric between the layers of a folded fluffy white towel and iron on a fairly hot setting. Use cooler settings if metallic thread is used. The towel will also help to protect any beads from being crushed.

Beads

Beads are used to embellish some of the designs, as they produce a lovely three-dimensional quality to the project. They replace the cross stitch and so take up one block of thread on Aida or two threads of fabric on evenweave. To attach a bead, use half a cross stitch so that it lies in the same direction as the top diagonal of the cross stitch. Come up at 1, pass the needle through the bead and come down at 2 (see Fig i). You can use beads to replace all the cross stitches of any design that contains whole cross stitches without any fractional stitches – just choose beads of the nearest match to the thread colour stated in the key.

Charms

Charms and buttons can also be added to any design to create a three-dimensional effect. These are attached using sewing cotton of the same colour as the fabric they are to be stitched onto.

Fig i

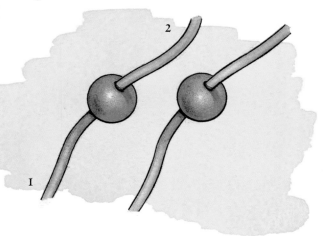

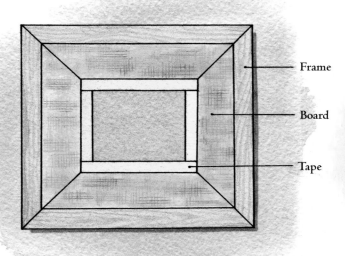

Frame

Board

Tape

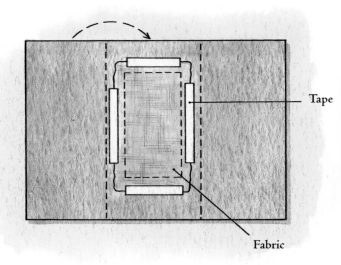

Tape

Fabric

Framing

Small pictures can be easily framed, without the need to take your work to a professional picture framer. Consider whether you require a mount before choosing the frame size, as this may mean you need a bigger frame. Cut a piece of cardboard the same size as the back of the frame. Attach double-sided tape along all four sides and fold the finished fabric with the wrong side facing around the board, making sure that the picture is central. Wadding can be used if needed and placed between fabric and board. To secure everything, tape the edges of the fabric to the board using masking tape to secure before placing in the frame (Fig j). Choosing acid-free materials will ensure that your stitching will be preserved for a long time. Decide if the glass you are to use is going to be ordinary glass or non-reflective. Non-reflective glass is the best choice in a room that is well lit, or near a window. After sandwiching the finished work between the glass and backing board seal the frame with gummed, brown paper (the kind used for parcels) to protect from moisture and dust. If you plan to hang the picture in a bathroom, seal with silicone sealant instead of gummed, brown paper. Never hang your framed work opposite a window, as strong sunlight will bleach the colours of the materials. It is important to allow plenty of extra fabric before starting to stitch to allow for framing a good 3 or 4in (7.6 or 10.2cm) on a medium-sized design. It will also mean that you are not limited to using a particular mount or frame size.

Mounting a card

Choose a three-fold card mount with a suitable size and shape aperture. Lay your work against a range of colours to see which best complements your work. Stick double-sided tape around the aperture of the card on the wrong side. Lay your work face up and place the card with the aperture centrally over your stitching and press into place; the tape will hold it secure. Trim the fabric, if necessary, to fit in the card. Place the card and stitching face down and stick the left-hand third over the fabric using double-sided tape to finish (Fig k).

Other methods of presentation

The designs in this book could be presented in several ways depending on your choice and the size of the finished design. There is a good range of products available including trinket pots, coasters and paperweights. Follow the manufacturer's instructions when using these. Remember, although I have made suggestions for the mounting of each project, do not be limited by them. The suppliers listed towards the back of the book offer a wide variety of products to experiment with.

Personalizing your stitching

Here is a simple alphabet and series of numbers for adding a personal touch to your stitching and gifts. For example, you may wish to embellish samplers and larger items with your initials and the year that you stitched them. I have deliberately omitted a thread key, as you can use any colour of thread to stitch with. All the letters and numbers use backstitch only.

Alphabet and numbers chart

Projects

Flower-pot Picture and Card

I like to see pots of flowers adorning patios and terraces –
they give instant colour and form, and look good in groups
wherever they are placed. This design is deceptively simple to
stitch because it is made up of smaller motifs. The design
contains whole cross stitches and backstitch, with a few
fractional stitches. If you feel daunted by the picture, stitch
the small card, first where I have substituted the three shades
of lavender for a variegated thread, to give subtle shading.
Just remember when using this type of thread to complete
each cross stitch before stitching the next, in order to achieve
the best effect.

Any of the motifs in this design can be stitched
individually to make many small gifts. Try stitching a flower
pot and mounting it in a key-ring design. To work out how
large the finished motif will be, see pages 11–12. Remember,
the fabric count can always be altered to make the design
smaller or larger. Using 28-count evenweave, instead of
Aida, and stitching over two strands of thread, will give the
same finished size.

Flower-pot picture

Method

1 Find the centre of the fabric and begin stitching here, following the chart. Work the cross stitches over one block of fabric, referring to the instructions on page 14 if necessary.

2 Use two strands of thread for cross stitch and one for backstitch, as indicated in the key.

Backstitch: pots 434, pale pink flowers in centre pot 603, stems on lavender 561, all other greenery 367, poppies 326, all other pink flowers including border flowers 601, and purple flowers 3746.

3 Once all the stitches have been completed, press the fabric and mount within the chosen frame. Refer to page 18 for tips on framing.

Materials

14-count white Aida, 11 x 13in (27.9 x 33cm) (Zweigart colour 100)
DMC stranded cotton, as listed in the key
Size 26 tapestry needle
Frame with aperture 7 x 9in (17.8 x 22.9cm)

Design size

6 x 7⅞in (15.2 x 20cm) at 14-count

Stitch count

84 x 111

Thread key

		DMC				DMC
f	Pink Lightest	963			Blue Violet Medium	340
6	Lavender Medium	210			Green Dark	986
∩	Green Light	368			Blue Violet Dark	3746
/	Yellow	744			Pink Deep	326
⬆	Terracotta Light	3856			Pink Dark	601
✦	Terracotta Medium	402		↔	Blue Violet Light	341
⬛	Tan	437		**Backstitch**		
◤	Brown Light	434		▬	Brown Light	434
H	Green Very Light	369		▬	Green	367
◪	Green	367		▬	Pink Medium	603
⚡	Pink Medium	603		▬	Jade Dark	561
⬚	Lavender Light	211		▬	Blue Violet Dark	3746
◣	Jade Dark	561		▬	Pink Deep	326
◀	Jade	562		▬	Pink Dark	601
×	Pink Light	605		**French knots**		
Σ	Terracotta Dark	3776		●	Blue Violet Dark	3746
!	White	Blanc				

Flower-pot card

Method

1   Find the centre of the fabric and begin stitching here, following the chart. Work the cross stitches over one block of fabric, referring to the instructions on page 14 if necessary.

2   Use two strands of thread for cross stitch and one for backstitch, as indicated in the key.

3   Once all the stitches have been completed press the fabric.

4   Mount the card within the square following the instructions on page 18.

Thread key	DMC			DMC
Purple	034*	**Backstitch**		
Jade	562	Jade Dark	561
Jade Dark	561	Brown Light	434
Terracotta Medium	402	*Oliver Twist	
Terracotta Dark	3776		

Materials

14-count white Aida, 6 x 6in (15.2 x 15.2cm)
   (Zweigart colour 100)
DMC stranded cotton, as listed in the key
Size 26 tapestry needle
Three-fold card blank with aperture
   3 x 3in (7.6 x 7.6cm)

Design size

2⅜ x 2⅜in (6.1 x 6.1cm) at 14-count

Stitch count

33 x 33

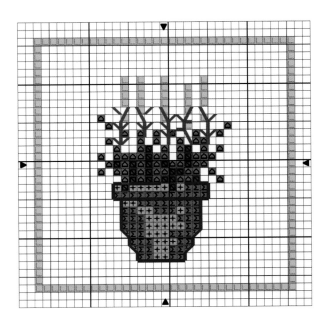

Butterfly Kitchen Set

Gardens encourage natural wildlife — I think butterflies, birds and insects are wonderful to see in any garden. Some plants attract them more than others, for instance the buddleia is often called the 'butterfly bush', because butterflies and bees are attracted to its purple or white flower-heads. Each of these butterfly designs are easy to stitch and are suitable for the beginner, just whole cross stitch and some backstitch is used. Either of the larger butterfly motifs could be stitched and attached to the front of a recipe notebook. The Aida band could be attached to a window blind or curtain tie-backs.

Butterfly tea-towel border

Method

1   Begin stitching 1in (2.5cm) from the left side of the Aida band. Following the chart, repeat the motif pattern until the desired length is achieved. It is a good idea to measure the tea towel and work out how many repeats you need before you start stitching in order to avoid mistakes. Work the cross stitches over one block of fabric, referring to the instructions on page 14 if necessary.

2   Use two strands of thread for cross stitch and one for backstitch, as indicated in the key.

3   After all the stitches have been completed, press the fabric and stitch to the right side of the tea towel using small running stitches, turning under the side edges for a neat finish.

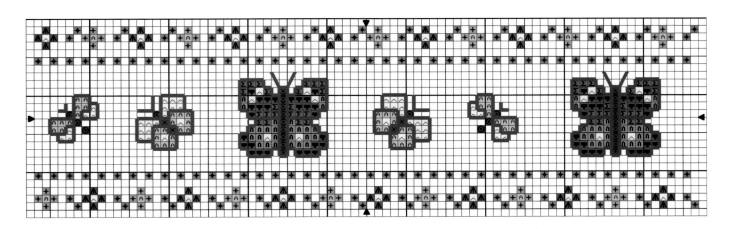

Materials

Aida band, 2in (5.1cm) wide x the length of a
   tea towel, plus 1in (2.5cm) for hemming
DMC stranded cotton, as listed in the key
Size 26 tapestry needle
Tea towel

Design size

1¾ x 6in (4.4 x 15.2cm) at 14-count

Stitch count

24 x 84

Thread key	DMC		DMC
Σ Brown Medium	611	∧ Yellow Light	3078
◉ Brown Dark	610	∧ Blue Violet Dark	3746
∩ Brown Light	612	✚ Lavender Dark	209
■ Red	666	**Backstitch**	
✦ Green	368	— Brown Dark	610
∩ Yellow	726		

Butterfly oven-mitt patch

Method

1   Find the centre of the fabric and begin stitching here, following the chart. Work the cross stitches over one block of fabric, referring to the instructions on page 14 if necessary.

2   Use two strands of thread for cross stitch and one for backstitch, as indicated in the key.

3   Remove a few threads around all four sides to obtain a frayed appearance.

4   Stitch the patch to the front of the oven mitt using small running stitches.

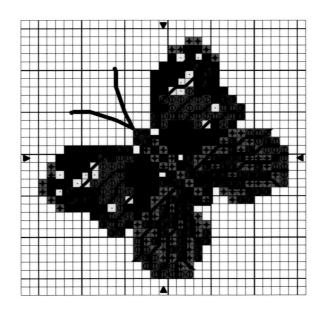

Materials

14-count white Aida, 4 x 4in (10.2 x 10.2cm)
  (Zweigart colour 100)
DMC stranded cotton, as listed in the key
Size 26 tapestry needle
Three-fold card with circular aperture of 2in
  (5.1cm) diameter

Design size

2⅜ x 2⅜in (6.1 x 6.1cm) at 14-count

Stitch count

33 x 33

Thread key	DMC		DMC
Red	666	**Backstitch**	
Cream	712	▬ Brown Darkest	3371
Brown Darkest	3371	**French knots**	
Brown Medium	840	● Brown Darkest	3371
Brown Dark	838		

Butterfly tea-cosy patch

Method

1 Find the centre of the fabric and begin stitching here, following the chart. Work the cross stitches over one block of fabric, referring to the instructions on page 14 if necessary.

2 Use two strands of thread for cross stitch and one for backstitch, as indicated in the key.

3 When all the stitches have been completed press the fabric.

4 Remove a few threads around all four sides to obtain a frayed appearance.

5 Stitch the patch to the front of the tea cosy using small running stitches.

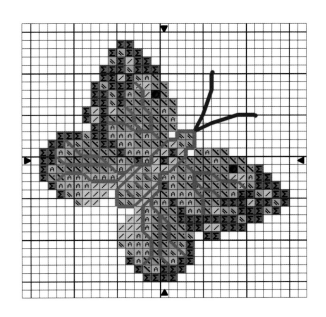

Materials

14-count white Aida, 5 x 5in (12.7 x 12.7cm)
  (Zweigart colour 100)
DMC stranded cotton, as listed in the key
Size 26 tapestry needle
Tea cosy

Design size

2⅛ x 2⅛in (5.4 x 5.4cm) at 14-count

Stitch count

29 x 29

Thread key	DMC		DMC
Yellow Dark	725	**Backstitch**	
Yellow Light	744	Brown Dark	898
Brown Dark	898	Brown Medium	613
Brown Light	613	**French knots**	
Brown Medium	611	Brown Dark	898
Yellow	726		

Summer Garland Stitcher's Set

This pretty garland design is presented on a pincushion, so it would make a lovely gift for a stitcher. The design could also be mounted in a three-fold card or small frame, which I have also shown. The scissor-keep completes the set, though the design could also be made into a gift tag. Both projects are suitable for the beginner, as they are simple and quick to stitch, containing whole cross stitches and backstitch only. Either can be stitched using evenweave fabric if you prefer: use 28-count stitched over two threads of fabric to give the same finished size.

Summer garland pincushion

Method

1   Find the centre of the fabric and start here, following the chart. Work the cross stitches over one block of thread, referring to the instructions on page 14 if necessary.

2   Use two strands of thread for cross stitch and one strand for backstitch as indicated in the key.

3   After all the stitches have been completed press the fabric.

4   Trim both pieces of fabric to 6in (15.2cm). With the right sides facing each other, stitch the two pieces of fabric together, leaving a seam allowance of ½in (1.3cm) all the way around and a small opening for turning and stuffing.

5   Turn the cushion back the right way and stuff using the wadding.

6   Slip-stitch cord around all four sides of the cushion, starting by inserting the beginning of the cord into the opening. When the cord has been stitched all the way around the cushion, insert the other end into the opening and slip-stitch the hole closed.

Materials

14-count white Aida, two pieces 7 x 7in (17.8 x 17.8cm) (Zweigart colour 100)
DMC stranded cotton, as listed in the key
Size 26 tapestry needle
Wadding and cord for finishing

Design size

3¾ x 3¾in (9.5 x 9.5cm) at 14-count

Stitch count

53 x 53

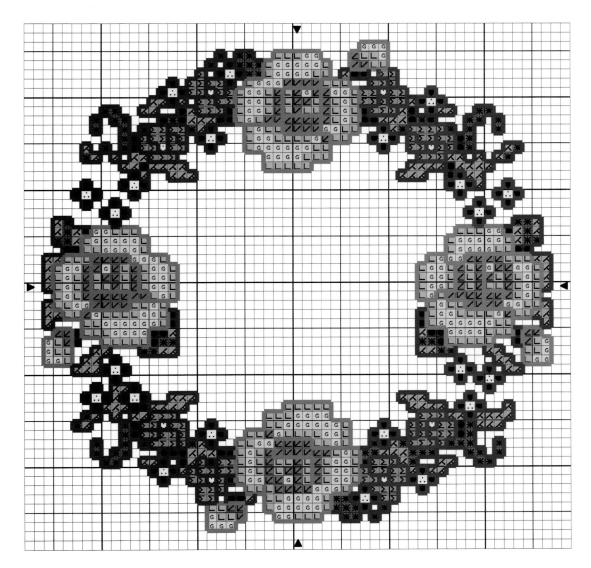

Thread key

	DMC			DMC
G Pink Lightest	818		Pink Medium	3326
Yellow Light	3823		Pink Dark	335
Jade Dark	561	**Backstitch**		
Green	368		Jade Dark	561
Jade	562		Blue Dark	792
Blue Dark	792		Pink Dark	335
Blue	794			

Summer garland scissor-keep

Method

1   Find the centre of the fabric and start here following the chart. Work the cross stitches over one block of thread, referring to the instructions on page 14 if necessary. Use two strands of thread for cross stitch and one strand for backstitch, as indicated in the key.

2   Once the stitches are complete press the fabric.

3   Trim both pieces of fabric to 4in (10.2cm) and, with right sides facing, stitch the two pieces of fabric together, leaving a seam allowance of ½in (1.3cm) all the way around and a small opening for turning and stuffing.

4   Turn the scissor-keep the right way and stuff using the wadding.

5   Slip-stitch cord around all four sides, starting at the opening, insert the beginning of the cord, make a large loop in the bottom corner for the scissors to be attached and a smaller loop in the top opposite corner. When the cord has been stitched all the way around, insert the other end into the opening and slip-stitch the hole closed.

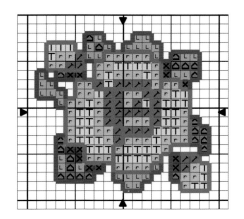

Materials

14-count white Aida, two pieces 4 x 4in
(10.2 x 10.2cm) (Zweigart colour 100)
DMC stranded cotton, as listed in the key
Size 26 tapestry needle
Wadding and cord for finishing

Design size

1¼ x 1¼n (3.2 x 3.2cm) at 14-count

Stitch count

18 x 17

Thread key	DMC		DMC
T Pink Lightest	818	◪ Pink Dark	335
r Pink Medium	3326	**Backstitch**	
✖ Jade Dark	561	▬ Jade Dark	561
L Green	368	▬ Pink Dark	335
⌂ Jade	562		

Lavender Keepsakes

Lavender is a popular herb-garden plant with the most wonderful scent, and is said to contain antiseptic and relaxing properties. This evergreen plant makes fragrant, thick hedging and forms neat rows in formal knot gardens. I do find it self-seeds around the garden — I see it growing in the strangest of places!

These pretty, delicate designs would make lovely gifts. The sachet could be made up into a card, or small picture if you prefer. The lavender-pot design is also suitable for stitching onto a gift tag or bag. Both projects are easy to stitch, containing only whole cross stitch and backstitch.

Lavender scented sachet

Method

1   Find the centre of the fabric and start here following the chart. Work the cross stitches over one block of fabric, referring to the instructions on page 14 if necessary.

2   Use two strands of thread for cross stitch and one for backstitch, as indicated in the key.

Backstitch the border using 3838, the stem detail using 561, the pot using 640 and the text and lavender flower detail using 333.

3   After all the stitches have been completed press the fabric.

Materials

14-count white Aida, 7 x 7in (17.8 x 17.8cm)
  (Zweigart colour 100)
DMC stranded cotton, as listed in the key
Size 26 tapestry needle
Cord or ribbon 24in (60cm) long

Design size

4 x 4in (10.2 x 10.2cm) at 14-count

Stitch count

56 x 56

Thread key

		DMC			DMC
6	Lavender Medium	210	~	Flesh	951
	Jade Dark	561	!	White Bright	B5200
	Purple	333	&	Blue	157
V	Blue Violet	155	**Backstitch**		
人	Green Light	3817	—	Jade Dark	561
◆	Green Medium	163	—	Purple	333
↖	Terracotta Light	3856	—	Brown	640
▲	Terracotta Dark	3776	—	Blue Medium	3839

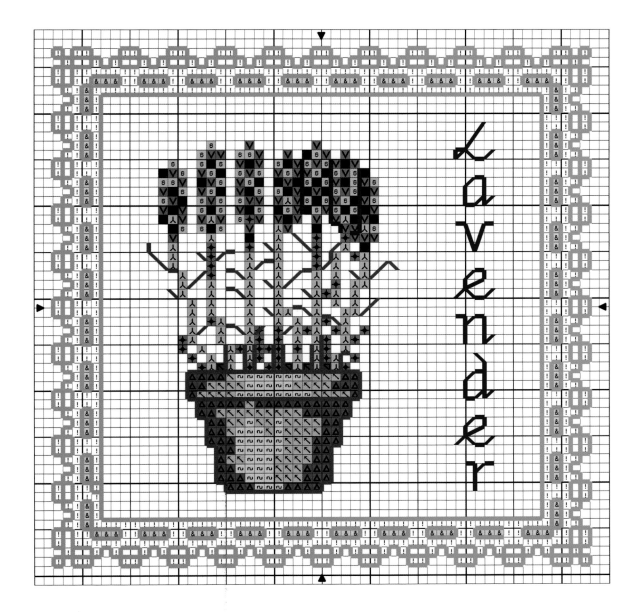

4 Ensuring the design is central, trim both pieces of fabric to 6 x 6in (15.2 x 15.2cm). With right sides facing, stitch the two pieces of fabric together leaving a seam allowance of ½in (1.3cm) all the way around and a small opening for turning and stuffing.

5 Turn the cushion the right way and stuff using the wadding.

6 Insert pot pourri into the opening.

7 Slip-stitch cord around all four sides of the cushion starting at the opening, inserting the beginning of the cord. When the cord has been stitched all the way around the cushion, insert the other end into the opening and slip-stitch the hole closed.

Lavender bookmark

Method

1 Fold the fabric in half. With the fold at the top find the centre of the half of this folded fabric and start here following the chart. Work the cross stitches over one block of fabric, referring to the instructions on page 14 if necessary.

2 Use two strands of thread for cross stitch and one for backstitch, as indicated in the key.

Backstitch the bow using 208, the border using 3838, the stem detail using 561 and the lavender flower detail using 333.

Materials

Aida band, 26 stitches wide by 12½in (31.8cm) (Zweigart E7107 white)
DMC stranded cotton, as listed in the key
Size 26 tapestry needle
Tassel

Design size

2 x 5¼in (5 x 13.3cm) at 14-count

Stitch count

26 x 74

3 After all the stitches have been completed press the fabric.

4 With right sides facing, fold the length of Aida band in half and draw a diagonal line from each edge (about 1½in (3.8cm) up from the bottom) to meet at the bottom in the centre stitch along these lines. Turn the fabric the right way.

5 Stitch down the sides of the fabric using small running stitches, leaving a small opening in the centre in which to attach the tassel.

6 Attach the tassel to the bottom of the bookmark using discreet stitches and slip-stitch the opening closed.

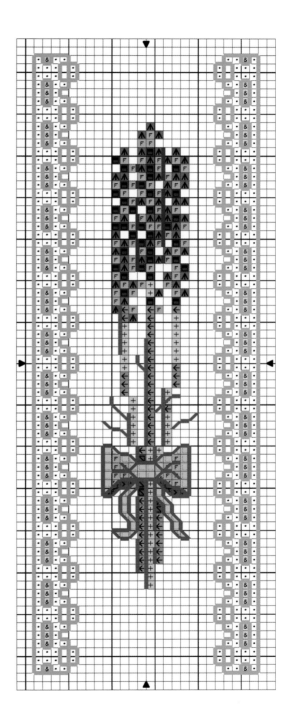

Thread key	DMC		DMC
Lavender Light	211	Jade Dark	561
Lavender Medium	210	Blue Violet	155
Lavender Dark	208	**Backstitch**	
White Bright	B5200	Lavender Dark	208
Purple	333	Purple	333
Blue	157	Blue Medium	3839
Green Light	3817	Jade Dark	561
Green Medium	3816		

Pansy Stationery

A member of the viola, or violet, family, the pansy features in gardens between late autumn and spring. The bright velvety petals appear in combinations of purples, blues, yellows and whites. The pansy is the birthday flower of June and in the Victorian language of flowers means 'thoughts', probably because the name 'pansy' is thought to derive from the French verb *penser*, to think.

These tasteful designs are very simple to stitch and suitable for anyone with little or no experience. The designs contain only whole cross stitch and a little backstitch. The motifs can be stitched onto any item, for example a key ring, luggage tag, or fridge magnet. I have chosen a card, bookmark and gift tag. You could also stitch an initial using backstitch into the centre of the design.

Pansy card

Method

1 Find the centre of the fabric and begin stitching here, following the chart. Work the cross stitches over one block of fabric, referring to the instructions on page 14 if necessary.

2 Use two strands of thread for cross stitch and one for backstitch, as indicated in the key.

3 After all the stitches have been completed, press the fabric and mount within your chosen card. Refer to instructions on page 18 if necessary.

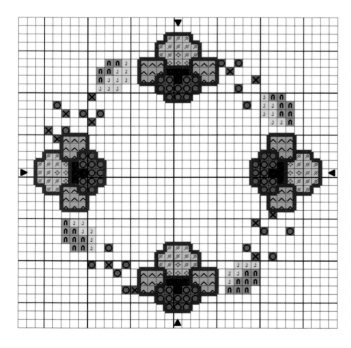

Thread key	DMC		DMC
✧ Yellow	726	✗ Green Dark	320
⬤ Blue Violet	340	⟋ Violet Light	3747
⌃ Blue Violet Light	341	■ Violet Dark	550
∩ Green Medium	368	**Backstitch**	
ɹ Green Light	369	▬ Blue Violet Dark	3746

Materials

14-count white Aida, 4 x 4in (10.2 x 10.2cm) (Zweigart colour 100)

DMC stranded cotton, as listed in the key

Size 26 tapestry needle

Three-fold card blank, with circular aperture 2½in (6.4cm) in diameter

Design size

2⅜ x 2⅜in (6.1 x 6.1cm) at 14-count

Stitch count

33 x 33

Pansy gift tag

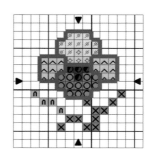

Method

1 Find the centre of the fabric and start here following the chart. Work the cross stitches over one block of fabric, referring to the instructions on page 14 if necessary.

2 Use two strands of thread for cross stitch and one for backstitch, as indicated in the key.

3 After all the stitches have been completed, press the fabric. Trim the fabric to just less than 1¾ x 1¾in (4.5 x 4.5cm), ensuring the design is centred.

4 Attach the fabric to the card front using either double-sided tape or a suitable glue. Thread the ribbon through the ready-punched hole.

Thread key	DMC		DMC
✧ Yellow	726	✗ Violet Light	3747
◎ Blue Violet	340	◖ Violet Dark	550
⋀ Blue Violet Light	341	**Backstitch**	
✕ Green Dark	320	— Blue Violet Dark	3746
∩ Green Medium	368		

Materials

14-count white Aida, 3 x 3in (7.6 x 7.6cm) (Zweigart colour 100)
DMC stranded cotton, as listed in the key
Size 26 tapestry needle
Two-fold blank gift tag
A piece of ribbon approx. 12in (30.5cm) long

Design size

⅞ x ⅞in (2.2 x 2.2cm) at 14-count

Stitch count

12 x 11

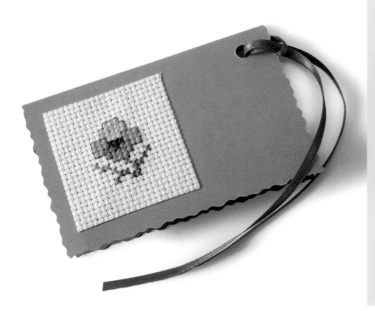

Pansy bookmark

Method

1 Find the centre of the fabric and start here following the chart. Work the cross stitches over one block of fabric referring to the instructions on page 14 if necessary.

2 Use two strands of thread for cross stitch and one for backstitch as indicated in the key.

3 After all the stitches have been completed press the fabric. Trim the fabric to allow for approximately four blocks of fabric on either side of the design and to within the same length of the card used. Attach the fabric to the card using either double-sided tape or suitable glue.

Thread key	DMC		DMC
Yellow	726	Violet Light	3747
Blue Violet	340	Violet Dark	550
Blue Violet Light	341	**Backstitch**	
Green Dark	320	Blue Violet Dark	3746
Green Medium	368		

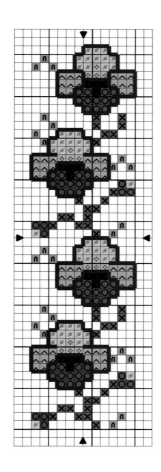

Materials

14-count white Aida, 3 x 8in (7.6 x 20.3cm)
  (Zweigart colour 100)
DMC stranded cotton, as listed in the key
Size 26 tapestry needle
Piece of card 2 x 7in (5.1 x 17.8cm)

Design size

⅞ x 3¼in (2.2 x 8.3cm) at 14-count

Stitch count

12 x 46

Knot-garden Set

Formal knot gardens could traditionally be seen outside stately homes, where armies of gardeners would have been needed to keep them in a constantly tidy state. Topiary hedges and bushes would have been clipped to perfection and there would have been perfectly placed benches to give the best views in a tranquil setting.

The picture design is very simple to reflect this, using only whole cross stitch and backstitch, with just a few three-quarter stitches for the shaping of the sundial in the picture. The flowers in the knot-garden border are made using multi-coloured thread to produce a unique effect. I have used one strand of perlé cotton, though you could use three strands of stranded cotton, which is available in the same colour if you wish.

The knot-garden concept has also been used to create a pincushion. You will notice how I have varied the stitching with the multi-coloured thread to achieve different results from the knot garden in the picture — all I have done is changed my direction of stitching.

The topiary-tree sachet contains whole cross-stitches and backstitch only, with attractive charms to add further interest. All three of these designs are simple — suitable for even the beginner to stitch and the charms give just the right finish, too. Paint the charms with clear acrylic varnish before attaching them as this will reduce the chance of them tarnishing with age.

Knot-garden picture

Method

1 Find the centre of the fabric and begin stitching here, following the chart. Work the cross stitches over one block of fabric, referring to the instructions on page 14 if necessary.

2 Use two strands of stranded thread and one strand of perlé cotton for cross stitch and one strand for backstitch, as indicated in the key.

Backstitch the bench, pots and bees using 3781, the sundial using 317 and the trees using 561.

3 After all the stitches have been completed press the fabric and attach the charms.

4 Mount within the chosen frame following the instructions on page 18 if necessary.

Materials

14-count white Aida, 7 x 9in (17.8 x 22.9cm) (Zweigart colour 100)
DMC stranded cotton
Anchor perlé cotton no. 5, as listed in the key
Size 26 tapestry needle
Suitable frame with aperture 7 x 5in (17.8 x 12.7cm)
Two butterfly charms

Design size

3⅝ x 5⅝in (9.2 x 14.3cm) at 14-count

Stitch count

51 x 79

Thread key

		DMC			DMC
⁄	Rainbow	1335*	Ɛ	Grey Light	415
◆	Iris	1325*	✳	Grey Medium	318
←	Green Medium	3816	⟋	Yellow 743	
◼	Jade Dark	561	**Backstitch**		
⋀	Tan	437	▬	Jade Dark	561
✚	Pink Variegated	48	▬	Brown	3781
◼	Brown	3781	▬	Grey Dark	317

*Anchor perlé cotton no. 5

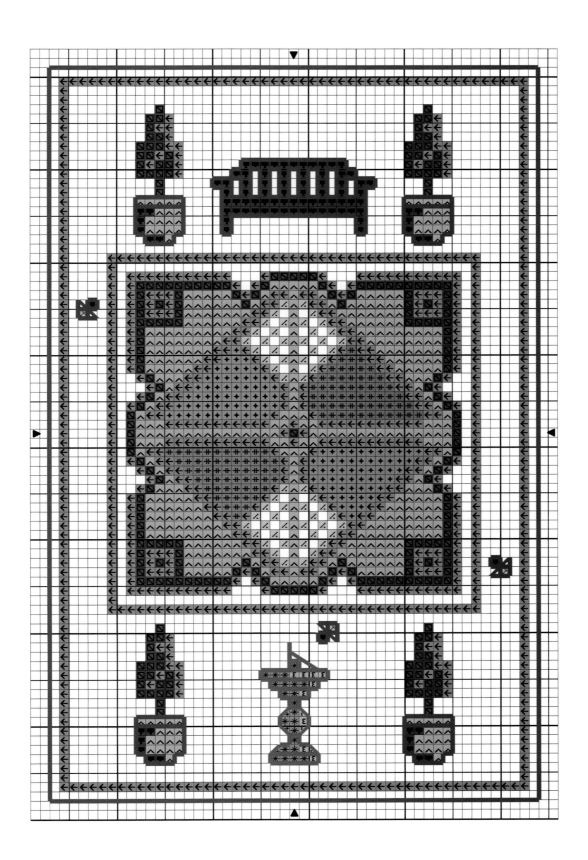

Knot-garden pincushion

Method

1   Find the centre of the fabric and start here following the chart. Work the cross stitches over one block of fabric, referring to the instructions on page 14 if necessary.

2   Use two strands of stranded cotton thread, and one strand of perlé cotton thread for the cross stitch, as indicated in the key. N.B. there is no backstitch in this design.

3   After all the stitches have been completed press the fabric and attach the charm.

4   Trim both pieces of fabric to 5 x 5in (12.7 x 12.7cm). With right sides facing, stitch the two pieces of fabric together leaving a seam allowance of ½in (1.3cm) all the way around and a small opening for turning and stuffing.

5   Turn the cushion the right way and stuff using the wadding.

6   Insert the beginning of the cord into the opening, and slip-stitch cord around all four sides of the cushion. When the cord has been stitched all the way around the cushion, insert the other end into the opening and slip-stitch the hole closed.

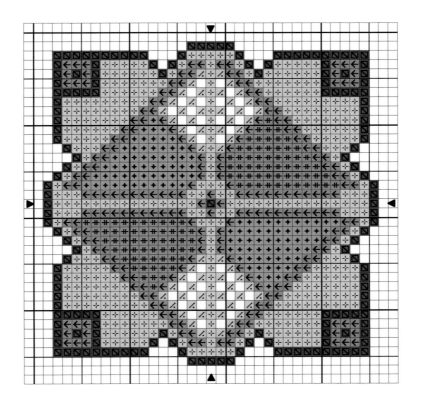

Materials

14-count white, Aida 7 x 9in (17.8 x 22.9cm)
  (Zweigart colour 100)
DMC stranded cotton, as listed in the key
Anchor perlé cotton no. 5, as listed in the key
Size 26 tapestry needle
Suitable frame with an aperture 7 x 5in
  (17.8 x 12.7cm)
Two butterfly charms

Design size

2½ x 2½in (6.4 x 6.4cm) at 14-count

Stitch count

35 x 35

Thread key

		DMC				DMC
∕.	Rainbow	1335*		◼	Jade Dark	561
◆	Iris	1325*		✛	Tan	738
←	Green Medium	3816		✛	Pink Variegated	48

*Anchor perlé cotton no. 5

Topiary-tree scented sachet

Method

1 Find the centre of the fabric and start here following the chart. Work the cross stitches over one block of fabric, referring to the instructions on page 14 if necessary.

2 Use two strands of thread for cross stitch and one for backstitch.

Materials

14-count white Aida, 5 x 5in (12.7 x 12.7cm)
  (Zweigart colour 100)
Two pieces of white fabric, 6 x 9in
  (15.2 x 22.9cm)
DMC stranded cotton, as listed in the key
Size 26 tapestry needle
Ribbon to tie the bag, 12in (30.5cm) long
Ribbon to trim, 40in (101.6cm) long
Two bee charms
Iron-on interfacing or Vilene (optional)

Design size

2⅞ x 2⅞in (7.3 x 7.3cm) at 14-count

Stitch count

40 x 40

3 Once all the stitches have been completed, press the fabric and then stitch the charms in place. Attach a lightweight iron-on interfacing and trim the fabric with the design central to 3 x 3in (7.6 x 7.6cm).

4 With the right sides together, stitch the two pieces of white fabric along the sides and bottom, leaving small gaps at the top of each side to thread the ribbon.

5 Sew a small hem along the top all the way around. Turn the bag the right way around, stitch the lace along the top and thread the ribbon through the top hem.

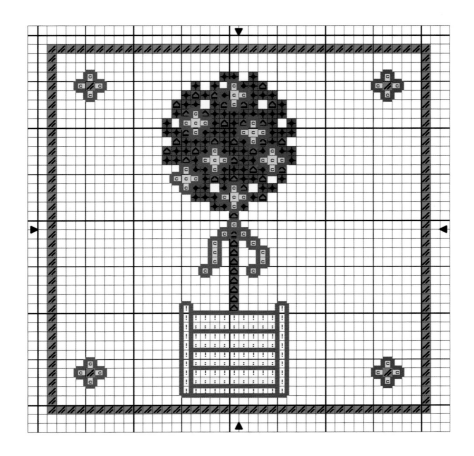

6 Stitch the patch to the front of the bag with small, neat stitches.

7 Finish the four sides of the bag and the top edge by decorating with a suitable ribbon. I have used DMC Fantasy Velum colour 5480.

8 For the finishing touch, fill the bag with dried lavender or pot pourri. The bag could be used as a gift bag.

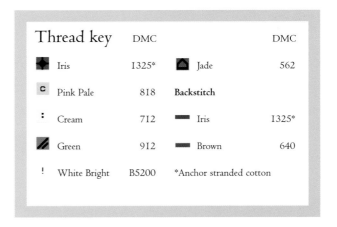

Thread key	DMC		DMC
Iris	1325*	Jade	562
c Pink Pale	818	**Backstitch**	
: Cream	712	— Iris	1325*
Green	912	— Brown	640
! White Bright	B5200	*Anchor stranded cotton	

Floral Samplers

I have designed these simple samplers so that they can be completed in just a few hours. All three are ideal first pieces for a beginner. Stitch the designs using evenweave fabric if you prefer a more rustic appearance, though 28-count over two threads of fabric will give the same size. The mini band sampler and floral sampler are quick and easy to stitch, and could be adapted if you wish. For example, try using different types of buttons.

The band sampler wall-hanging is a slightly larger sampler that has been made into a wall-hanging using bell pulls. The design is stitched onto Aida band and is finished with a pretty pink edging. The bands could be stitched onto other items, too. I have introduced half cross stitch which is really a diagonal (the first or last part of a cross stitch). See the instructions on page 15 if you are about working this stitch.

Mini band sampler

Method

1 Find the centre of the fabric and begin stitching here, following the chart. Work the cross stitches over one block of fabric, referring to the instructions on page 14 if necessary.

2 Use two strands of thread for cross stitch as indicated in the key. (There is no backstitch in this design.)

3 Once all the stitches have been completed, press the fabric and mount within the chosen frame. Refer to page 18 if necessary for tips on framing.

Materials

14-count white Aida, 6 x 8in (15.2 x 20.3cm)
  (Zweigart colour 100)
DMC stranded cotton, as listed in the key
Size 26 tapestry needle
Frame with an aperture 3 x 5in (7.6 x 12.7cm)

Design size

2½ x 4½in (6.4 x 11.4cm) at 14-count

Stitch count

35 x 63

Thread key

		DMC				DMC
	Lavender Light	211	+	Green Bright		907
P	Blue Light	827	+	Yellow		726
	Blue Violet	340	V	Green		368
^	Blue Electric	996	═	Violet		554
■	Blue Lavender Dark	3838		Green Medium		367

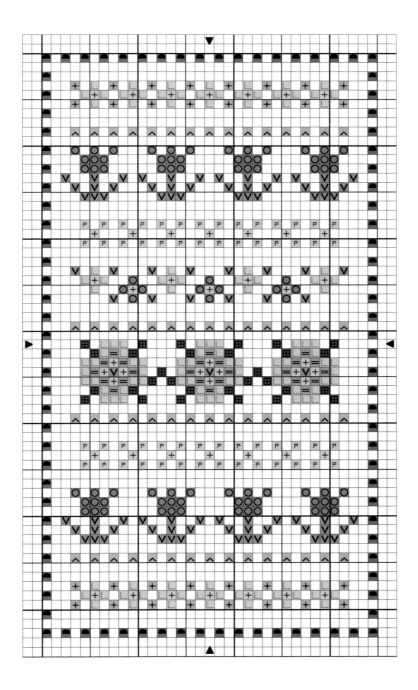

Band sampler wall-hanging

This is a slightly larger sampler that has been made into a small wall-hanging using bell pulls. The design is stitched onto Aida band and is finished with a pretty pink edging. The bands and motifs could be stitched onto other items, too. I have introduced half cross stitch which is really a diagonal line (the first or last part of a cross stitch) see the instructions on page 15 if you are unsure how to work this stitch. The design is suitable for beginners.

Method

1   Find the centre of the fabric and begin stitching here, following the chart. Alternatively you could start at the top and work across in rows if you prefer. Work the cross stitches over one block of fabric, referring to the instructions on page 14 if necessary.

2   Use two strands of thread for cross stitch, half cross stitch and one for backstitch, as indicated in the key.

3   Once all the stitches have been completed, press the fabric.

4   Hem the top and bottom edges allowing a 1in (2.5cm) seam allowance.

5   Thread the hangings through the top and bottom edges.

Materials

White Aida band, 54 stitches x 14in (35.6cm)
(Zweigart available from DMC)
DMC stranded cotton, as listed in the key
Size 26 tapestry needle
A pair of bell pulls

Design size

3¼ x 10¾in (8.3 x 27.3cm) at 14-count

Stitch count

45 x 150

Thread key

		DMC				DMC
■	Green Medium	320		═	Violet Medium	155
■	Mauve Medium	3607		■	Violet Dark	333
▨	Mauve Light	3608		**Half cross stitch**		
✦	Green Light	369		H	Green Light	369
◇	Green Medium	368		⋒	Green Medium	368
6	Mauve Lightest	3609		**Backstitch**		
U	Yellow	745		▬	Green Dark	320
✕	Lavender Light	211		▬	Violet Dark	333

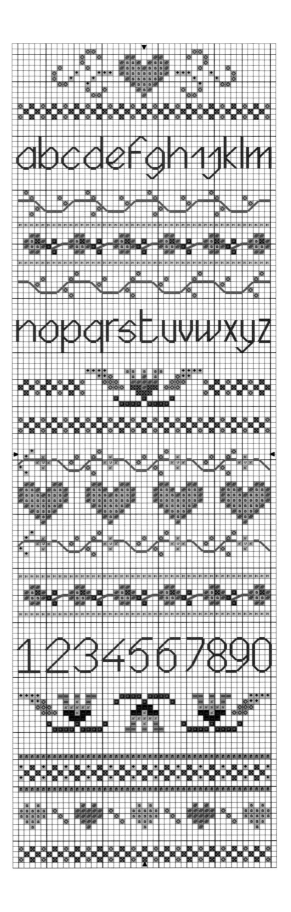

Alphabet sampler

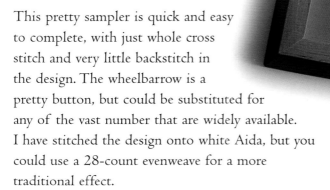

This pretty sampler is quick and easy to complete, with just whole cross stitch and very little backstitch in the design. The wheelbarrow is a pretty button, but could be substituted for any of the vast number that are widely available. I have stitched the design onto white Aida, but you could use a 28-count evenweave for a more traditional effect.

Materials

14-count white Aida, 12 x 12in
   (30.5 x 30.5cm) (Zweigart colour 100)
DMC stranded cotton, as listed in the key
Size 26 tapestry needle
Wheelbarrow button (available from DMC)
Frame with aperture 8 x 8in (20.3 x 20.3cm)
   and suitable mount

Design size

5⅞ x 5⅞in (14.9 x 14.9cm) at 14-count

Stitch count

83 x 83

Thread key

		DMC			DMC
=	Blue Violet	340	◣	Pink Dark	602
j	Blue Violet Light	3747	A	Yellow	726
H	Green Light	164	⅄	Mauve	210
∴	Yellow Pale	3078	**Backstitch**		
∩	Green Medium	368	—	Blue Violet	340
▪	Beige Dark	640	—	Green Light	164
◣	Pink Medium	604	—	Beige Dark	640
f	Pink Light	963			

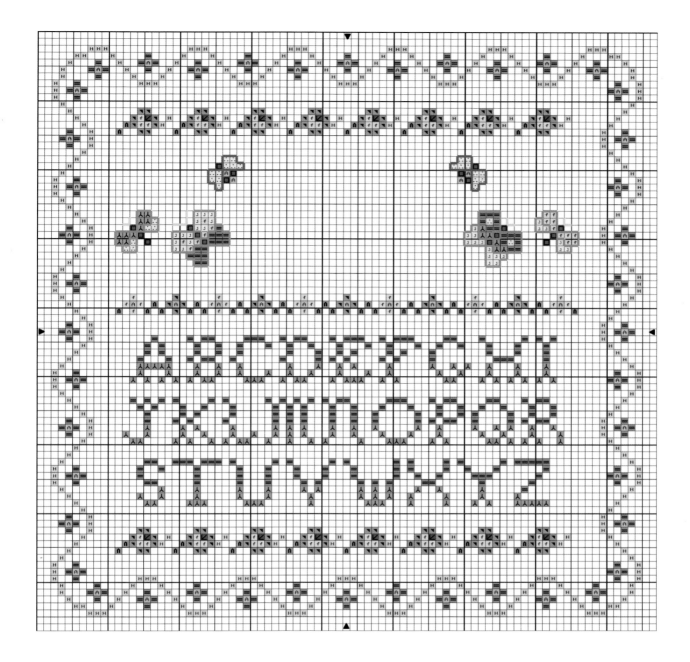

Method

1 Find the centre of the fabric and begin stitching here, following the chart. Work the cross stitches over one block of fabric, referring to the instructions on page 14 if necessary.

2 Use two strands of thread for cross stitch and one for backstitch, as indicated in the key.

3 Once all the stitches have been completed, press the fabric and attach the button using a suitable sewing thread.

4 Mount within the chosen frame. Refer to page 18 for tips on framing if necessary.

Rose Gifts

The rose is a particularly well-loved flower, being traditionally given as a symbol of love and affection. It is the birthday flower for the month of October, and has been appreciated by people the world over since ancient times for its colour, scent and medicinal properties. The Greeks named the flower and were the first to grow it in their gardens. They also wrote poems about it and painted its likeness on temple walls. Cleopatra was said to have seduced Mark Antony in a throne room filled knee-deep with rose petals. These designs can be stitched as individual items, or you could choose a selection to give as a coordinated set.

Rose picture

The rose picture is a pretty design – the simple border gives the impression that the roses are tumbling out of the picture. Whole cross stitches and backstitch are used in the foreground, while cross stitch with one strand of thread is used in the background. I have stitched the design using evenweave to it greater depth, but because there are no fractional stitches, the design can be stitched using 14-count Aida if you prefer.

Materials

28-count white evenweave Quaker cloth,
  12 x 10in (30.5 x 25.4cm)
    (Zweigart colour 100)
DMC stranded cotton, as listed in the key
Size 26 tapestry needle
Frame with aperture 6 x 8in (15.2 x 20.3cm)

Design size

6⅛ x 4⅞in at 14-count

Stitch count

86 x 69

Thread key	DMC			DMC
⫷ Pink	761		◼ Green Dark	986
♡ Pink Lightest	819		**Cross stitch: one strand**	
∧ Flesh Palest	3770		✚ Misty Green Light	3817
6 Peach Light	353		◻ Misty Green Dark	3815
✖ Green Medium Dark	320		**Backstitch: one strand**	
∩ Green Medium	368		▬ Pink Deep	3328
H Green Light	369		▬ Peach Deep	351
╱ Peach Medium	352		▬ Green Deep	319
✚ Pink Medium	760			

Method

1 Find the centre of the fabric and begin stitching here, following the chart. Work the cross stitches over two threads of fabric, referring to the instructions on page 14 if necessary.

2 Use two strands of thread for cross-stitch roses and foreground leaves, and one strand for the cross-stitch background leaves and all backstitch, as indicated in the key.

Backstitch the leaves using 319, the pink rose and buds using 3328 and the peach rose with 351.

3 Once all the stitches have been completed, press the fabric and mount within the chosen frame. Refer to page 18 if necessary for tips on framing.

Rose bookmark

This rose bookmark is a simple project to stitch, containing only whole cross stitch and backstitch. Stitch it as a treat for yourself or a gift for a friend.

Method

1 Fold the Aida fabric in half. With the fold at the top, find the centre of this half of fabric and start here following the chart. Work the cross stitches over one block of fabric, referring to the instructions on page 14 if necessary.

2 Use two strands of thread for cross stitch and one for backstitch, as indicated in the key.

3 Once all the stitches have been completed, press the fabric.

4 With wrong sides facing, fold the Aida band in half ensuring the design is centred. The raw edges should be at the bottom. Turn each raw edge under about ½in (1.3cm) and slip-stitch to neaten.

5 Slip-stitch down the sides.

6 Fold the ribbon in half and stitch to the front of the bookmark. Stitch the ribbon rosebud in place over the top of the fold using small discreet stitches.

Thread key	DMC		DMC
Green Dark	367	Pink Dark	601
Green Medium	368	Pink Light	963
Green Light	369	**Backstitch**	
Pink	604	Green Dark	367
Pink Medium	602	Pink Dark	601

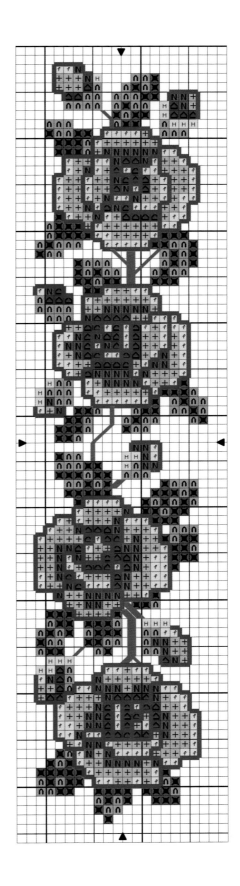

Materials

White Aida band, 26 stitches wide by 14in (35.6cm) in length (Zweigart E7107, available from DMC)

DMC stranded cotton, as listed in the key

Size 26 tapestry needle

Length of ribbon, approx. 12in (30.5cm) long

Ribbon rosebud (optional)

Design size

1¼ x 5⅞in (3.2 x 15cm) at 14-count

Stitch count

18 x 82

Beaded rose handbag mirror

The beaded rose handbag mirror design is produced entirely out of beads to give a lovely three-dimensional quality. You could replace the beads with cross stitch – every bead would represent a cross stitch. Use two strands of thread of the same colours used for attaching the beads for best results. I have mounted the rose into a handbag mirror, though you could use a three-fold card or trinket pot if you prefer.

Method

1 Find the centre of the fabric and begin stitching here, following the chart. Work the beads over one block of fabric using half cross stitch to attach them, referring to the instructions on page 15 if necessary.

2 Use one strand of thread to attach the beads, matching it as indicated in the key.

3 Once all the stitches have been completed, mount within the mirror, referring to the manufacturer's instructions. If you need to press the finished design, place in a thick towel and be careful not to crush the beads.

Materials

14-count white Aida, 5 x 5in (12.7 x 12.7cm)
  (Zweigart colour 100)
DMC stranded cotton
DMC beads, as listed in the key
Size 26 tapestry needle
Beading needle
Handbag mirror
Iron-on interfacing or Vilene

Design size

1½ x 1⅝in (3.8 x 4cm) at 14-count

Stitch count

21 x 22

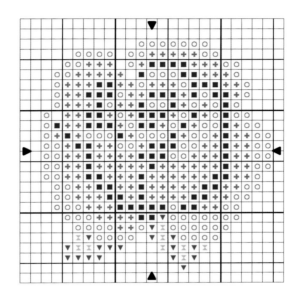

4   I would recommend that you use lightweight iron-on interfacing or Vilene to back the work. This will stop it from fraying before cutting it out to fit the mirror. Use the acetate disc provided as a template. Position the acetate centrally over the stitching and draw around it with a pencil, then cut out following the pencil line carefully. Assemble according to the manufacturer's instructions.

Attach beads using the stranded cotton as follows:

v2 02 666	- 666	I strand
v2 02 3777	- 304	I strand
v4 02 666	- 350	I strand
v4 03 702	- 702	I strand
v4 03 704	- 704	I strand

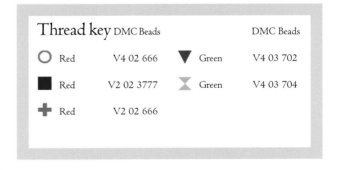

Thread key DMC Beads

O	Red	V4 02 666	▼ Green	V4 03 702
■	Red	V2 02 3777	✕ Green	V4 03 704
✚	Red	V2 02 666		

Rose alphabet

The letters could be stitched individually as monograms or together to form a whole name for a bedroom-door plaque, though my example is stitched as a coaster. Just substitute the letter 'A' for the letter of your choice, centre it within the gingham border so that there is equal spacing around it. All 26 letters of the alphabet are given in the chart. There are only whole cross stitches and no backstitches used in this design, making it perfect for the beginner. I have chosen 18-count Aida so that the design will fit into the coaster, but for other purposes you could use 14-count Aida which will make the finished item slightly larger.

Materials

18-count white Aida, 6 x 6in (15.2 x 15.2cm) (Zweigart colour 100)
DMC stranded cotton, as listed in the key
Size 26 tapestry needle
Square coaster
Iron-on interfacing or Vilene (optional)

Design size

3⅛ x 3⅛in (7.9 x 7.9cm) at 18-count

Stitch count

57 x 57

Coaster
Method

1   Find the centre of the fabric and begin stitching here, following the chart. Work the cross stitches over one block of fabric, referring to the instructions on page 14 if necessary.

2   For the letters use two strands of thread for cross stitch as indicated in the key, for the gingham border use one strand of thread for the cross stitches. There is no backstitch used in this design.

3   Once all the stitches have been completed, press the fabric and mount within the coaster, following the manufacturer's instructions.

4   I would recommend that you use lightweight iron-on interfacing or Vilene to back the work. This will stop it from fraying before cutting it out to fit the coaster.

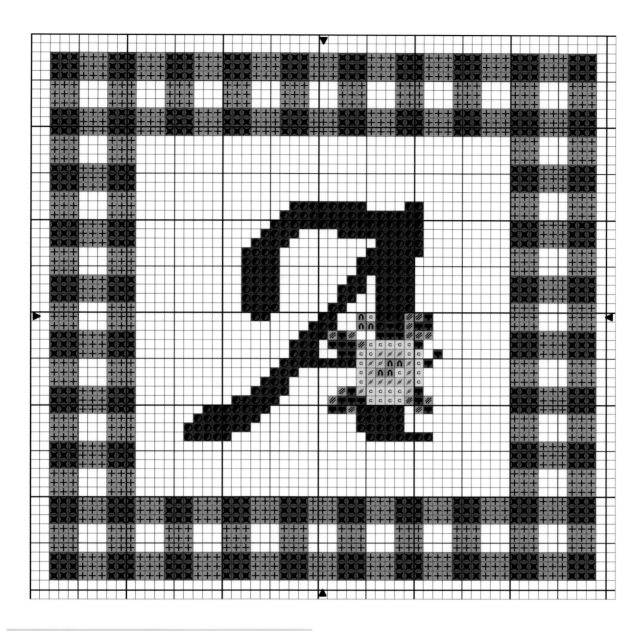

Thread key   DMC

Coaster (above)

		DMC			DMC
c	Pink Palest	818	✚	Green Light	368*
⌀	Pink Medium	3716	◖	Pink Deepest	326
∩	Pink Deep	899	◼	Green Dark	986
◪	Green Medium	367*	⫽	Green	989

* One strand

Thread key   DMC

Rose alphabet (page 80)

		DMC			DMC
◖	Pink Deepest	326	c	Pink Palest	818
⌀	Pink Medium	3716	◼	Green Dark	986
∩	Pink Deep	899	⫽	Green	989

Rose trinket pot

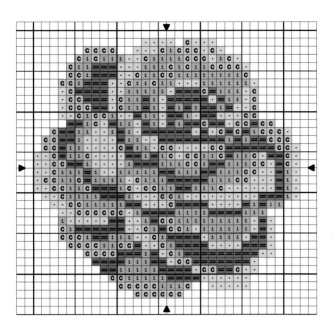

Method

1 Find the centre of the fabric and begin
stitching here, following the chart. Work the cross
stitches over one block of fabric, referring to the
instructions on page 14 if necessary.

2 Use two strands of thread for cross stitch as
indicated in the key.

3 Once all the stitches have been completed, press
the fabric and assemble according to manufacturer's
instructions.

4 I would recommend that you use lightweight
iron-on interfacing or Vilene to back the work. This
will prevent it from fraying before cutting it out to
fit the trinket pot. Use the acetate disc provided as
a template. Position the acetate centrally over the
stitching and draw around it with a pencil, then cut
out following the pencil line carefully. Assemble
according to the manufacturer's instructions.

Thread key	DMC			DMC
· Pink Palest	819	▬ Pink Deep		961
C Pink Pale	818	1 Pink Medium		3326

Rose candle

Method

1 Find the centre of the fabric and begin stitching here, following the chart. Work the cross stitches over one block of fabric, referring to the instructions on page 14 if necessary.

2 Use two strands of thread for cross stitch and one for backstitch, as indicated in the key.

3 Repeat the motif until the required length is reached; this will depend on the size of the candle.

4 Once all the stitches have been completed, press the fabric and wrap around the candle fold under the edges where they meet to obtain a neat edge. Secure with either a suitable glue or double-sided tape.

Remember to remove the band when burning the candle for safety reasons.

Materials

Aida band, 26 stitches x circumference of the chosen candle plus overlap of about 1in (2.5cm)

DMC stranded cotton, as listed in the key

Size 26 tapestry needle

Candle

Design size

1½ x 3⅜in (3.8 x 8.6cm) at 14-count, repeated to desired length

Stitch count

21 x 47

Thread key

		DMC			DMC
L	Pink Pale	818	▲	Jade	562
∅	Pink	3716	**Backstitch**		
Ⅱ	Pink Deep	961	—	Jade	562
ε	Jade Light	563			

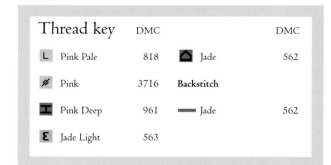

Rose sampler

Method

1 Start at the top of the chart and complete each row before working the next, following the chart, measure 3¼in (8.3cm) down and 3¼in (8.3cm) across the fabric to start. This should place the design centrally on the fabric. Work the cross stitches over two threads of fabric, referring to the instructions on page 14 if necessary.

Materials

28-count white evenweave, 10 x 16in (25.4 x 40.6cm)

DMC stranded cotton, as listed in the key

Size 26 tapestry needle

Beading needle

Suitable frame and optional mount

Pink ribbon, ⅛in (3mm) wide and 7in (17.8cm) long

A selection of pink and green silk ribbon, 3mm wide to make the roses

Design size

3¾ x 9½in (9.5 x 24.2cm) at 14-count

Stitch count

52 x 133

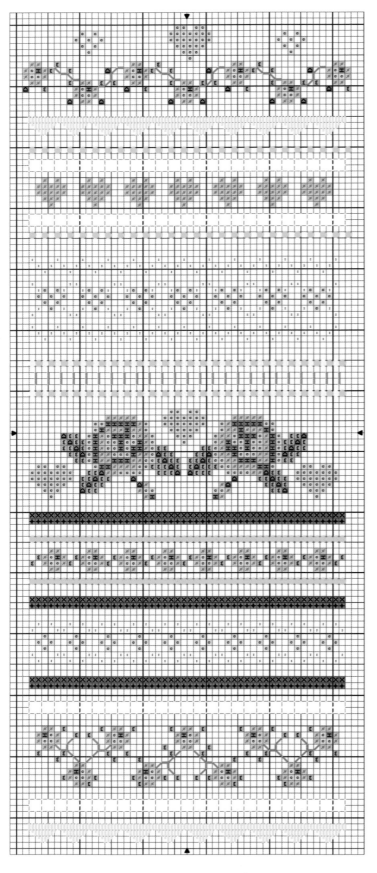

2 Use two strands of thread for cross stitch and one for backstitch and all other stitches as indicated in the key, attach the beads with one strand of DMC stranded cotton shade 818. Secure the ribbon using one strand of DMC 961.

3 For instructions on how to make the ribbon roses using the spider's web method, see page 16.

4 Once all the stitches have been completed, press the fabric very carefully and mount within the chosen frame. Refer to page 18 if necessary for tips on framing.

Thread key	DMC		DMC
c Pink Pale	818	**Backstitch**	
∅ Pink	3716	— Pink Pale	818
I Pink Deep	961	— Pink Deep	961
ε Jade Light	563	— Jade	562
⬠ Jade	562	White	Blanc
: White	Blanc	**Beads: Mill Hill Seed**	
Half cross stitch: forward facing		Dusty Rose	02005
		White	00479
✕ Pink Deep	961		
Half cross stitch: backward facing			
◆ Pink Deep	961		

Charm Designs

These pretty designs can be completed in just a few hours, perhaps set aside an evening to complete each one. The charms give a lovely finish to the designs. Designed with even the beginner in mind using whole cross stitches and some backstitch, they are sure to appeal to the more advanced stitcher, too.

Heart card

Method

1 Find the centre of the fabric and begin stitching here, following the chart. Work the cross stitches over one block of fabric, referring to the instructions on page 14 if necessary.

2 Use two strands of thread for cross stitch as indicated in the key.

3 Once all the stitches have been completed, press the fabric and attach the charm using white sewing cotton.

4 Mount within the card following the instructions on page 18.

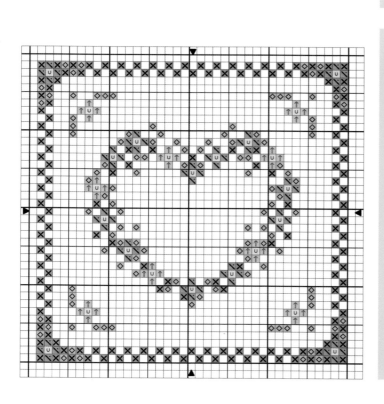

Thread key

		DMC			DMC
⬆	Pink	605	◇	Green Bright	704
◥	Cerise	3806	U	Yellow	726
✖	Green Dark	702			

Materials

14-count white Aida, 6 x 6in (15.2 x 15.2cm) (Zweigart colour 100)
DMC stranded cotton, as listed in the key
Size 26 tapestry needle
Three-fold card blank with 3 x 3in (7.6 x 7.6cm) aperture
Heart charm

Design size

2¾ x 2¾in (7 x 7cm) at 14-count

Stitch count

39 x 39

Formal-garden card

Method

1 Find the centre of the fabric and begin stitching here, following the chart. Work the cross stitches over one block of fabric, referring to the instructions on page 14 if necessary.

2 Use two strands of thread for cross stitch and one for backstitch, as indicated in the key.

3 Once all the stitches have been completed, press the fabric and attach the charm using white sewing cotton.

4 Mount within the card following the instructions on page 18.

Materials

14-count white Aida, 6 x 6in (15.2 x 15.2cm)
  (Zweigart colour 100)
DMC stranded cotton, as listed in the key
Size 26 tapestry needle
Three-fold card blank with 3 x 3in
  (7.6 x 7.6cm) aperture
Dragonfly charm

Design size

2¾ x 2¾in (7 x 7cm) at 14-count

Stitch count

39 x 39

Thread key	DMC		DMC
▥ Lavender Blue	3838	✚ Lavender Dark	209
◇ Green Bright	704	▦ Turquoise	958
◖ Green Dark	702	**Backstitch**	
↑ Lavender Blue Light	3840	▬ Lavender Blue	3838

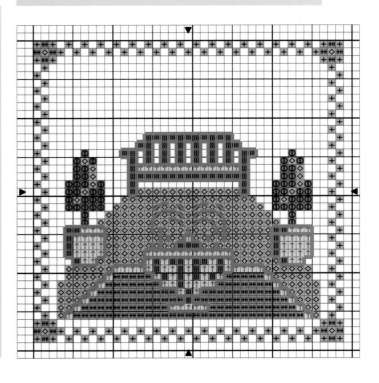

Flower-pot card

Method

1 Find the centre of the fabric and begin stitching here, following the chart. Work the cross stitches over one block of fabric, referring to the instructions on page 14 if necessary.

2 Use two strands of thread for cross stitch and one for backstitch, as indicated in the key.

3 Once all the stitches have been completed, press the fabric and attach the charm using white sewing cotton.

4 Mount within the card following the instructions on page 18.

Thread key	DMC		DMC
Ĵ Lavender Light	211	＋ Yellow	726
＋ Lavender Dark	209	◐ Green Dark	702
◣ Blue Violet Dark	3746	⬆ Pink	605
◥ Cerise	3806	**Backstitch**	
◇ Green Bright	704	— Blue Violet Dark	3746

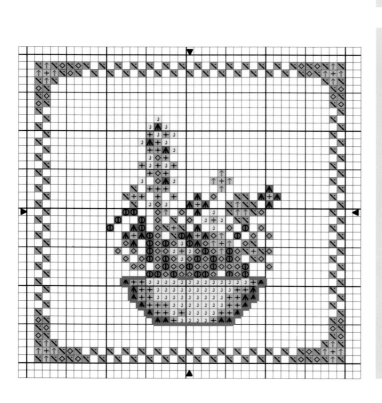

Materials

14-count white Aida, 6 x 6in (15.2 x 15.2cm) (Zweigart colour 100)
DMC stranded cotton, as listed in the key
Size 26 tapestry needle
Three-fold card blank with 3 x 3in (7.6 x 7.6cm) aperture
Butterfly charm

Design size

2¾ x 2¾in (7 x 7cm) at 14-count

Stitch count

39 x 39

Birdhouse notebook

Method

1 Find the centre of the fabric and begin stitching here, following the chart. Work the cross stitches over one block of fabric, referring to the instructions on page 14 if necessary.

2 Use two strands of thread for cross stitch and one for backstitch, as indicated in the key.

3 Once all the stitches have been completed, attach the charm using white sewing cotton.

4 Trim the fabric to 3½ x 3½in (8.9 x 8.9cm).

5 Attach the patch to the front of the notebook using double-sided tape or suitable glue.

Thread key	DMC		DMC
⬆ Pink	605	+ Yellow	726
◥ Cerise	3806	6 Lavender	210
~ Blue Violet Light	3747	✕ Green Dark	702
N Blue	807	**Backstitch**	
═ Blue Violet	340	— Blue Violet Dark	3746
◇ Green Bright	704		

Materials

14-count white Aida, 6 x 6in (15.2 x 15.2cm) (Zweigart colour 100)
DMC stranded cotton, as listed in the key
Size 26 tapestry needle
Notebook
Bird charm

Design size

2¾ x 2¾in (7 x 7cm) at 14-count

Stitch count

39 x 39

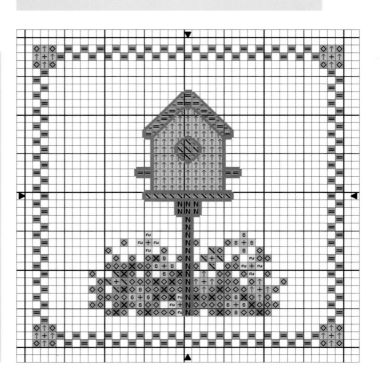

Vegetable-garden Sampler and Gifts

Planning and maintaining a vegetable garden can be an immensely enjoyable and rewarding activity, from designing the layout to harvesting the fruits of your labour. I have chosen the most popular of vegetables for these samplers. The gifts are quick to stitch and any keen gardener would be delighted to receive them. The designs use whole cross stitch, three-quarter cross stitch and some backstitch, and so might suit stitchers with a little experience. Beginners could try the vegetable notebook as a starting point. I have chosen to stitch the designs using Aida and evenweave – either could be used for each project.

Sampler picture

Method

1 Find the centre of the fabric and begin stitching here, following the chart. Work the cross stitches over one block of fabric, referring to the instructions on page 14 if necessary.

2 Use two strands of thread for cross stitch and one for backstitch, as indicated in the key.

3 Once all the stitches have been completed, press the fabric and mount within the chosen frame. Refer to page 18 if necessary for tips on framing.

Materials

14-count white Aida, 9 x 11in (22.9 x 27.9cm)
  (Zweigart colour 100)
DMC stranded cotton, as listed in the key
Size 26 tapestry needle
Frame with aperture 6 x 8in (15.2 x 20.3cm)

Design size

4½ x 6⅝in (11.4 x 16.8cm) at 14-count

Stitch count

63 x 92

Thread key

		DMC				DMC
⠒	Grey Medium Dark	318		╬	Pink Deep	347
A	Grey Light	762		▪	Red Dark	816
♡	White	Blanc		◩	Brown	3790
S	Pink Medium	3328		D	Grey Dark	317
◥	Orange	741		⅄	Grey Medium Light	415
■	Brown Dark	3021		**Backstitch**		
G	Green Light	3348		▬	Red Dark	816
■	Green Dark	319		▬	Black	310
M	Green Medium	3346				

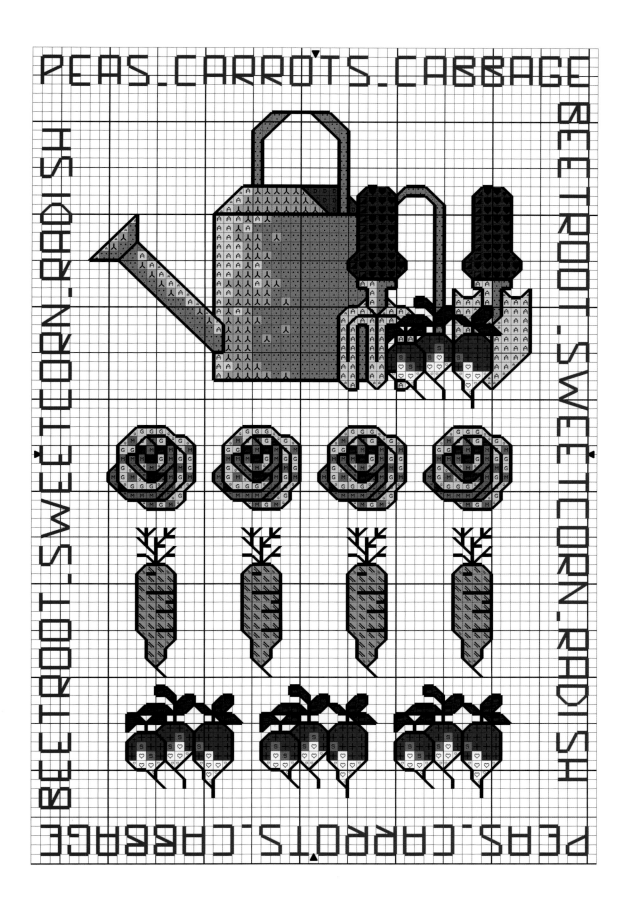

Key holder

Method

1 Find the centre of the fabric and start here following the chart. Work the cross stitches over one block of fabric, referring to the instructions on page 14 if necessary.

2 Use two strands of thread for cross stitch as indicated in the key.

3 Once all the stitches have been completed, press the fabric.

4 Trim both pieces of fabric and felt to 5 x 3½in (12.7 x 8.9cm). With right sides facing, stitch the two pieces together leaving a seam allowance of ½in (1.3cm) all the way around and a small opening for turning and stuffing.

Materials

14-count white Aida, 7 x 5in (17.8 x 12.7cm) (Zweigart colour 100)
A piece of felt, 7 x 5in (17.8 x 12.7cm)
DMC stranded cotton, as listed in the key
Size 26 tapestry needle
Wadding for stuffing
Cord, approx. 38in (1m) long
Tassel (optional)

Design size

3¼ x 1⅝in (8.2 x 4.1) at 14-count

Stitch count

45 x 23

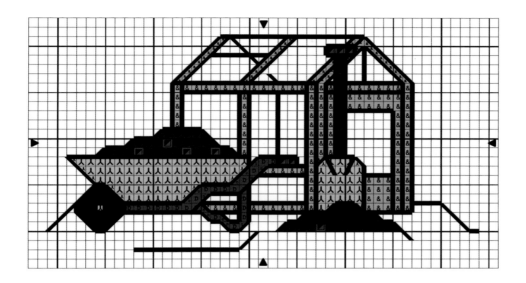

5 Turn the cushion the right way and stuff using the wadding.

6 Slip-stitch cord around all four sides of the cushion starting at the opening. Insert the beginning of the cord into the opening. Make a large loop in one corner to attach the key. When the cord has been stitched all the way around the cushion, insert the other end into the opening and slip-stitch the hole closed. You might like to add an extra touch by attaching a tassel of your choice.

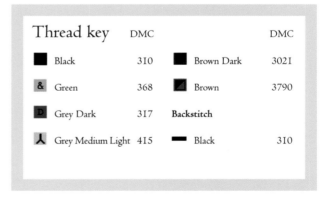

Thread key

		DMC			DMC
■	Black	310	■	Brown Dark	3021
&	Green	368	◪	Brown	3790
D	Grey Dark	317	**Backstitch**		
⅄	Grey Medium Light	415	▬	Black	310

Gardener's card

Method

1 Find the centre of the fabric and begin stitching here, following the chart. Work the cross stitches over one block of fabric, referring to the instructions on page 14 if necessary.

2 Use two strands of thread for cross stitch and one for backstitch, as indicated in the key.

3 After all the stitches have been completed press the fabric and mount within the card. Refer to page 18 if necessary for tips on mounting.

Materials

14-count white Aida, 7 x 6in (17.8 x 15.2cm)
   (Zweigart colour 100)
DMC stranded cotton, as listed in the key
Size 26 tapestry needle
Three-fold card blank with oval aperture

Design size

3¼ x 2¼in (8.2 x 5.7cm) at 14-count

Stitch count

46 x 32

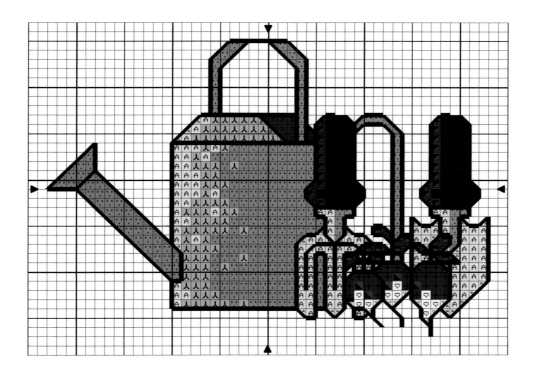

Thread key

		DMC				DMC
⊡	Grey Medium Dark	318	♡	White		Blanc
A	Grey Light	762	◼	Pink Medium		3328
◼	Brown Dark	3021	◪	Green Dark		319
◪	Brown	3790	◼	Pink Deep		347
◪	Grey Dark	317	**Backstitch**			
⅄	Grey Medium Light	415	▬	Black		310

Vegetable-garden journal

Method

1   Find the centre of the fabric and begin stitching here, following the chart. Work the cross stitches over two threads of fabric, referring to the instructions on page 14 if necessary.

2   Use two strands of thread for cross stitch and one for backstitch, as indicated in the key.

3   Once all the stitches have been completed press the fabric.

4   Trim the fabric to 4 x 4in (10.2 x 10.2cm). Cut a square piece of decorative paper about 5 x 5in (12.7 x 12.7cm) and attach to the underside of the design using double-sided tape.

5   Attach the patch to the front of the journal using double-sided tape or a suitable glue.

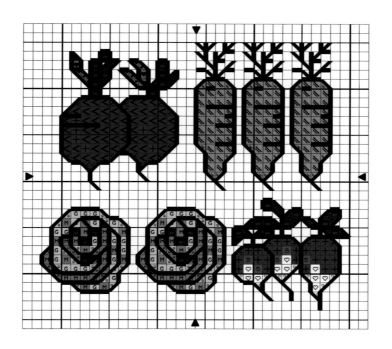

Materials

28-count white evenweave, 5 x 5in
  (12.7 x 12.7cm) (Zweigart colour 100)
DMC stranded cotton, as listed in the key
Size 26 tapestry needle
Notebook
Selection of decorative papers (optional)

Design size

2¼ x 2⅛in (5.7 x 5.4cm) at 14-count

Stitch count

32 x 29

Thread key

		DMC			DMC
✚	Pink Deep	347	◥	Orange	741
▦	Green Dark	319	♡	White	Blanc
◀	Red Dark	816	S	Pink Medium	3328
♥	Green	367	**Backstitch**		
G	Green Light	3348	▬	Black	310
M	Green Medium	3346			

Vegetable-garden motifs

Here is a selection of vegetable-garden motifs for you to stitch onto gifts and for designing your own samplers. If you are making a sampler, re-draw the motifs using graph paper and arrange them onto another page of graph paper until you have a pattern that you are happy with. Once you have glued the motifs in place, you can work from this chart to stitch the design. To work out the finished size of the design, divide the number of squares the design takes up on paper by the fabric count that you are going to use. For example, if your design is 28 x 42 squares of graph paper on 14-count fabric, this will result in the finished design being 2 x 3in (5.1 x 7.6cm). Don't forget to leave plenty of excess fabric on all four sides for framing. You can mix and match these designs with the fruit motifs on page 123 and the floral motifs on page 169.

Thread key	DMC		DMC
✦ Orange	740	◣ Garnet	816
▦ Tan	436	◥ Tangerine	741
人 Grey Light	415	♡ White	Blanc
▼ Bright Green Medium	702	⑤ Pink	3328
■ Bright Green Dark	699	⠶ Grey Medium	318
⋒ Bright Green	704	U Autumn Gold Light	3855
▣ Red	321	✛ Autumn Gold	3854
✳ Yellow	744	⠭ Tan Light	738
♥ Green Medium	367	**Backstitch**	
& Green	368	— Black	310
L Yellow Pale	3078	**French knots**	
✚ Deepest Pink	347	● Black	310
▬ Green Dark	319		

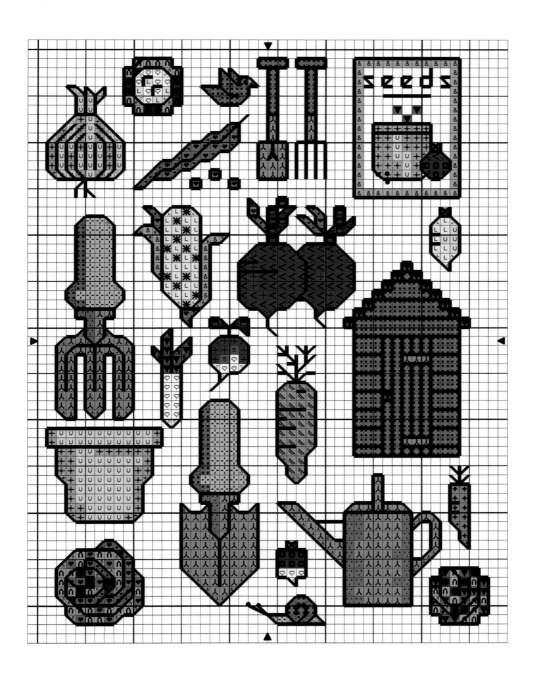

Autumn Leaves Stationery

There is nothing to match the beauty of golden leaves strewn in soft drifts in a woodland landscape. These attractive gifts are inspired by autumn leaves – the fantastic colours give a lovely warmth to the designs. I have chosen rayon threads and stitching paper to give a modern feel to these designs, which are very simple but effective. Snuggle up by the fire and enjoy making this set!

Leaf paperclip pot

Thread key

	DMC			DMC
Backstitch			Tan	436
Copper	922		Brown	433

Materials

14-count white Aida, 3 x 3in (7.6 x 7.6cm)
  (Zweigart colour 100)
DMC stranded cotton, as listed in the key
Size 26 tapestry needle
Mimi 'Fun Pot' (available from Framecraft)
Paperclips
Iron-on interfacing or Vilene (optional)

Design size

1⅛ x 1in (2.8 x 2.5cm) at 14-count

Stitch count

16 x 14

Method

1   Find the centre of the fabric and begin stitching here, following the chart.

2   Use one strand of thread for the backstitch (there is no cross stitch), as indicated in the key.

3   After all the stitches have been completed press the fabric back with a light weight iron-on interfacing or Vilene. Remove the cardboard disc from within the lid of the pot and use as a template. Centralize the design before drawing around and cutting it out. Assemble following the manufacturer's instructions.

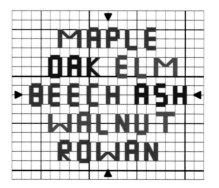

Leaf notelet

Method

1 Find the centre of the paper and begin stitching here (measure do not fold), following the chart.

2 Use two strands of thread for both the cross stitch and backstitch as indicated in the key. Take care not to fold the paper.

3 Once all the stitches have been completed, trim the paper to within one stitch on all sides, taking care not to snip any stitches.

4 Cut out a piece of handmade paper, in the shape of a whole leaf. Cut the hessian to slightly larger than the paper and stick behind the paper using either double-sided tape or suitable glue.

5 Stick the hessian-backed paper and the finished design onto the front of the card, leaving even borders. Finish by wrapping the gold thread around the front of the card several times (ensuring the card can open correctly) and tie in a knot.

Materials

14-count white stitching paper, 2½ x 3½in (6.4 x 8.9cm)
DMC stranded cotton, as listed in the key
Anchor marlitt, as listed in the key
Size 26 tapestry needle
Two-fold card blank
Handmade stitching paper (available from good craft stores)
Hessian or similar fabric
Gold-stranded cotton or similar to decorate

Design size

1⅛ x 2⅜in (2.8 x 6.1cm) at 14-count

Stitch count

16 x 33

Thread key DMC

♥ Coffee   1037*

Backstitch

▬ Brown   433

*Anchor marlitt

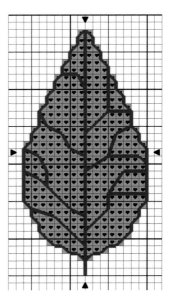

Leaf photograph album

Method

1 Find the centre of the fabric and begin stitching here, following the chart.

2 Use two strands of thread for the cross stitch and backstitch leaf veins, and one strand of thread for the backstitch text border, as indicated in the key.

3 Once all the stitches have been completed, press the fabric and trim to about 4in (10.2cm), removing a few strands of fabric from all four sides to give a frayed appearance.

4 If you are using handmade paper, as I have, cut the pieces out slightly larger than the fabric and attach the fabric centrally to the paper using double-sided tape.

5 Attach to the front of the photograph album using double-sided tape or a suitable glue.

Materials

18-count Rustico Aida, 5 x 5in
  (12.7 x 12.7cm) (Zweigart)
DMC stranded cotton, as listed in the key
Size 26 tapestry needle
Photograph album
Handmade paper (optional)

Design size

2⅝ x 3⅜in (6.7 x 8.6cm) at 18-count

Stitch count

48 x 47

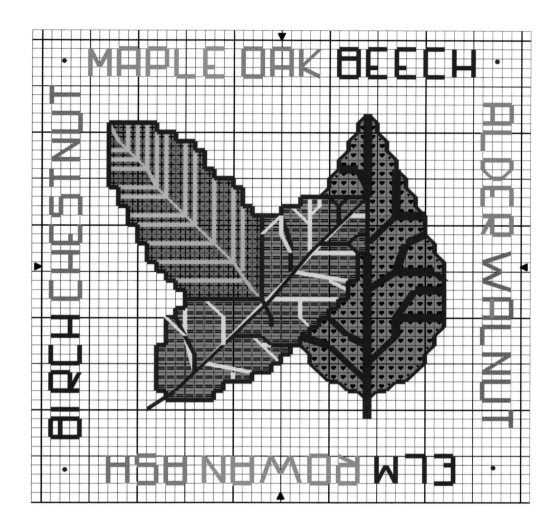

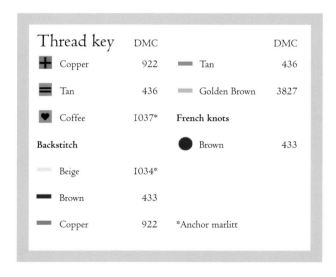

Thread key

		DMC				DMC
✚	Copper	922		▬	Tan	436
▬	Tan	436		▬	Golden Brown	3827
♥	Coffee	1037*		**French knots**		
Backstitch				●	Brown	433
▬	Beige	1034*				
▬	Brown	433				
▬	Copper	922		*Anchor marlitt		

Fruit Wall-hanging and Gifts

The fruit wall-hanging is suited to a stitcher with more experience, although only whole cross stitch and a small amount of backstitch is used, there is some blending of thread, this is where one strand of each of the two colours are used in the same needle (often called tweeding). Look closely at the key to see where this occurs. The result is more natural shading but requires no extra skill to achieve.

The cherry picture is more suitable for the beginner; any of the fruit could be stitched within the square border, just ensure the fruit is placed centrally. You could in fact stitch all four fruit as separate pictures rather than a wall hanging. Try stitching the border using a green variegated thread; DMC do a nice selection.

For the recipe book I have used the apple chart but you could choose any of the four designs.

The honey and jam jar covers will add a special touch to your breakfast table, and are quick projects to stitch. Alternatively, you could use the fruit motifs for different flavours of jar, or display them as I have shown, on items such as fridge magnets, notebooks and key rings.

Fruit wall-hanging

Method

1 Find the centre of the fabric and start here following the chart. Work the cross stitches over one block of fabric, referring to the instructions on page 14 if necessary.

2 Use two strands of thread for cross stitch, and one for backstitch as indicated in the key.

Backstitch cherry shadows in 3685, peaches and pears in 3778, branch shadows in 839 and leaf details and apples in 3345.

3 After all the stitches have been completed press the fabric.

Materials

14-count white Aida, 10 x 22in
  (25.4 x 55.9cm) (Zweigart colour 100)
Backing fabric, 10 x 22in (25.4 x 55.9cm)
DMC stranded cotton, as listed in the key
Size 26 tapestry needle
A pair of bell pulls, approx. 6½in
  (16.5cm) wide

Design size

4⅞ x 17in (12.4 x 43.2cm) at 14-count

Stitch count

68 x 238

Thread key

		DMC				DMC
♡	Pink Pale	819		Avocado Green	471
◇	Yellow	745		Pale Avocado Green	472
+	Flesh	950	◆	Golden Brown	977
V	Terracotta Light	3779	∩	Green	368
▲	Terracotta Medium	3778		Brown Medium	840
!	White Bright	B5200		Green Medium Dark	367
▬	Green Dark	3345		Rose	3354
▬	Brown	839		Plum	3685
Z	Green Medium	3347	◉	Dark Rose	3350
Σ	Khaki + Dark Flesh	3051 + 407	2	Spice	3825
←	Dark Flesh	407	▪	Yellow + Spice	745 + 3825
▪	Yellow + Terracotta Light	745 + 3779	**Backstitch**		
7	Terracotta Light + Medium	3779 + 3778	—	Terracotta Medium	3778
✕	Khaki	3051	—	Green Dark	3345
P	Pale Avocado + Golden Brown	472 + 977	—	Brown	839
r	Pale Laurel Green	772	—	Plum	3685

4 With right sides of the backing fabric and finished work facing, stitch down either side, making the finished piece just under 6in (15.2cm) in width to allow for the bell pull to fit. Make sure the design is central. Press the seams and turn the right way out.

5 Neaten the bottom and top edges. Fold the bottom and top edges over about 1in (2.5cm) and slip-stitch to secure (ensuring that the top and bottom borders are the same distance away from the edge of the fabric as the sides are). Remove one end of each bell pull and thread through the top and bottom edges.

I recommend that you use a thread sorter when stitching as there are several colours which are similar in shade.

Cherry picture

Materials

14-count white, Aida 9 x 9in (22.9 x 22.9cm)
   (Zweigart colour 100)
DMC stranded cotton, as listed in the key
Size 26 tapestry needle
Frame 6 x 6in (15.2 x 15.2cm) with a
   suitable mount

Design size

5 x 5in (12.7 x 12.7cm) at 14-count

Stitch count

68 x 68

Method

1   Find the centre of the fabric and start here following the chart. Work the cross stitches over one block of fabric referring to the instructions on page 14 if necessary.

2   Use two strands of thread for cross stitch, and one for backstitch as indicated in the key.

3   After all the stitches have been completed press the fabric and mount within the chosen frame. See page 18 for tips on framing.

Thread key

		DMC			DMC
∧	Pink Pale	819	◥	Rose	3354
✕	Green Medium Dark	367	■	Plum	3685
◼	Green Dark	3345	◉	Dark Rose	3350
◼	Brown	839	**Backstitch**		
r	Pale Laurel Green	772	▬	Green Dark	3345
∩	Green	368	▬	Brown	839
◆	Brown Medium	840	▬	Plum	3685

Apple recipe book

Method

1   Find the centre of the fabric and start here following the chart. Work the cross stitches over one block of fabric, referring to the instructions on page 14 if necessary.

2   Use two strands of thread for cross stitch and one for backstitch as indicated in the key.

3   After all the stitches have been completed press the fabric.

Thread key	DMC			DMC
◆ Golden Brown	977	⌐	Pale Laurel Green	772
◇ Yellow	745	✛	Avocado Green	471
■ Green Dark	3345	↗	Pale Avocado Green	472
■ Brown	839	**Backstitch**		
Z Green Medium	3347	—	Green Dark	3345
✖ Khaki	3051	—	Brown	839
P Pale Avocado Green + Golden Brown 472 + 977				

Materials

14-count white Aida, 9 x 9in (22.9 x 22.9cm) (Zweigart colour 100)
DMC stranded cotton, as listed in the key
Size 26 tapestry needle
Notebook or folder
Iron-on interfacing or Vilene

Design size

5 x 5in (12.7 x 12.7cm) at 14-count

Stitch count

68 x 68

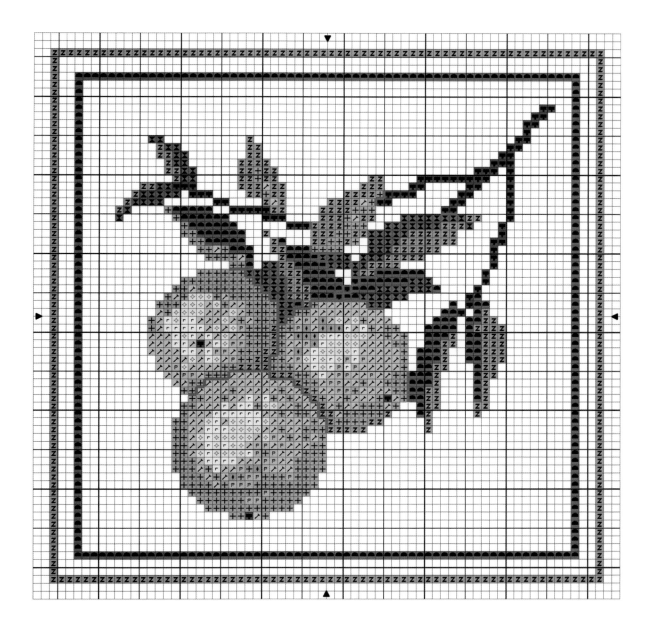

4 Trim the fabric to 6 x 6in (15.2 x 15.2cm).
Cut a piece of iron-on interfacing slightly larger
than the fabric and iron to the back of the fabric,
this will help to stop the edges from fraying. Trim
the fabric to 5 x 5in (12.7 x 12.7cm) or to within
five rows of fabric on all four sides.

5 Attach the patch to the front of the recipe
book using double-sided tape or a suitable glue.

Honey jar cover

There is nothing nicer than the taste of home-made honey and jam, and these jar covers would give a special touch to plain jars. You can also use the covers over the top of bought preserves to give a traditional look to your kitchen. Try experimenting with some of the motifs on the next pages for different flavours of jam. Here I have included honey and strawberry.

Materials

14-count white Aida, 5 x 5in (12.7 x 12.7cm)
  (Zweigart colour 100)
DMC stranded cotton, as listed in the key
Size 26 tapestry needle
Ribbon and lace to trim about 40in (1m) of
  each should be enough for both jars
Iron-on interfacing or Vilene (optional)

Design size

1⅜ x 1⅜in (3.5 x 3.5cm) at 14-count

Stitch count

20 x 20

Stitch both designs in the same way.

Thread key	DMC		DMC
⬆ Lavender	3840	✕ Green	702
⦀ Lavender Dark	3838	↺ Pale Yellow	3823
A Yellow	726	**Backstitch**	
■ Black	310	▬ Black	310
◢ Orange	741		

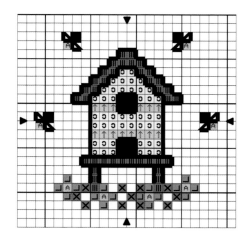

Strawberry jam-jar cover

Method

1 Find the centre of the fabric and begin stitching here, following the chart.

2 Work the cross stitches over one block of fabric, referring to the instructions on page 14 if necessary.

3 Use two strands of thread for cross stitch and one for backstitch as indicated in the key.

4 After all the stitches have been completed press the fabric, I recommend that you use lightweight iron-on interfacing to stiffen the fabric and help prevent the edges from fraying.

5 Using the jar lid as a template cut out a circle slightly larger than the lid of the jar. Stitch the lace around the edge of the lid neatly and then place over the top of the jar, I recommend that you use deep lace for a better fit. Secure with ribbon.

Thread key	DMC			DMC
✚ Red Dark	817		**A** Yellow	726
◑ Red	666		. Cream	746
◣ Green Pale	472		**Backstitch**	
◩ Green	470		▬ Black	310

Materials

14-count white Aida, 5 x 5in (12.7 x 12.7cm) (Zweigart colour 100)
DMC stranded cotton, as listed in the key
Size 26 tapestry needle
Ribbon and lace to trim, about 40in (1m) of each should be enough for both jars
Iron-on interfacing or Vilene (optional)

Design size

1¼in (3.2cm) diameter at 14-count

Stitch count

17 x 17

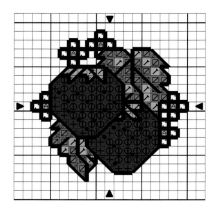

Fruit motifs and gifts

Here I have produced some small motifs that could be used for many different things. You could stitch the fruit designs onto jam jar covers as shown on pages 120–121. I have also chosen to use a fridge magnet, notebook and key ring as examples. You could use them for any number of items. To work out how big the finished design will be refer to pages 11–12. I have included an alphabet on page 19 so that you can personalize any gift you make.

Thread key	DMC			DMC
Red Dark	304		Lavender	209
Red	666		Violet Dark	552
Pink	760		Blue Violet	333
Raspberry Pink	3832		Topaz	725
Green	989		Darkest Brown	3371
Green Light	368		Beige	822
Green Dark	986		Green Bright	704
Gold	834	**Backstitch**		
Brown	610		Red Dark	304
Cream	746		Green Light	368
Yellow Pale	727		Green Dark	986
Yellow	726		Brown	610
Warm Yellow	743		Cream	746
Warm Yellow Pale	745		Brown Dark	433
Tangerine	742		Blue Violet	333
Orange	741		Darkest Brown	3371
Brown Dark	433			

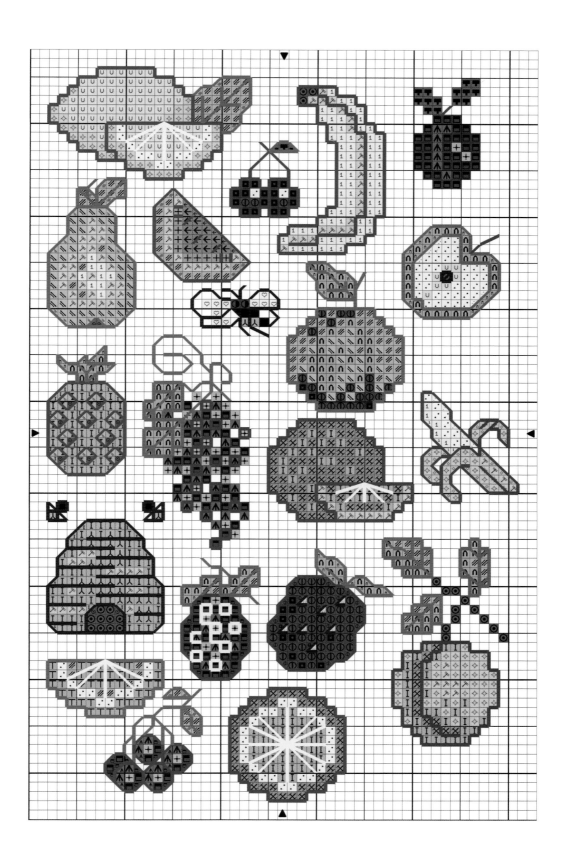

Lemon fridge-magnet and grape key-ring

Materials for lemon fridge-magnet

28-count Cashel linen in 'Baby Blue'
  (Zweigart colour 562), 4 x 3in
  (10.2 x 7.6cm)
DMC stranded cotton, as listed in the key
Size 26 tapestry needle
Fridge magnet
Iron-on interfacing or Vilene (optional)

Design size

1½ x ⅞in (3.8 x 2.2cm) at 14-count

Stitch count

21 x 12

Materials for grape key-ring

28-count Brittney in 'Sky Blue' (Zweigart
  colour 501), 3 x 4in (7.6 x 10.2cm)
DMC stranded cotton, as listed in the key
Size 26 tapestry needle
Key ring
Iron-on interfacing or Vilene (optional)

Design size

1 x 1⅝in (2.5 x 4.1cm) at 14-count

Stitch count

14 x 23

Method

1 Work both the designs in the same way. Find the centre of the fabric and begin stitching here, following the chart. Work the cross stitches over two threads of fabric, referring to the instructions on page 14 if necessary.

2 Use two strands of thread for cross stitch and one for backstitch, as indicated in the key.

3 Once all the stitches have been completed press the fabric and mount within the fridge magnet or key ring following the manufacturer's instructions.

4 I would recommend that you use lightweight iron-on interfacing or Vilene to back the work to stop it from fraying before cutting it out to fit the fridge magnet or key ring.

Peach notebook

Materials

28-count Cashel linen in 'Mint' (Zweigart
   colour 633), 4 x 5in (10.2 x 12.7cm)
DMC stranded cotton, as listed in the key
Size 26 tapestry needle
Small notebook

Design size

1 x 1¾in (2.5 x 4.4cm) at 14-count

Stitch count

13 x 23

Method

1   Find the centre of the fabric and begin
stitching here, following the chart. Work the cross
stitches over two threads of fabric, referring to the
instructions on page 14 if necessary.

2   Use two strands of thread for cross stitch and
one for backstitch, as indicated in the key.

3   After all the stitches have been completed press
the fabric and mount within the notebook using
the same method as you would for a three-fold card
– see page 18 if necessary.

Poppy Picture and Stationery

The poppy is a favourite of mine — today there are over 100 species of poppy in existence, the best-loved of all is the common field poppy, *Papaver rheos*, which grows almost like a weed, along roadsides, in hedges and speckled through fields of corn. Poppies have a long and fascinating history; garlands of the flower have been found in Egyptian tombs dating back to the pharaohs. It is also, of course, a well-known symbol of remembrance for the soldiers who gave their lives in World War I.

I have designed this common poppy for even the beginner to stitch; there are only whole cross stitches in this design and no backstitch. I have included a few French knots, but you could replace these with seed beads if you prefer. I have stitched the poppy using 14-count Aida, though 28-count evenweave would also be suitable, stitched over two blocks of thread.

Poppy picture

Materials

14-count white Aida, 7 x 9in (17.8 x 22.9cm)
 (Zweigart colour 100)
DMC stranded cotton, as listed in the key
Size 26 tapestry needle
Frame with aperture 5 x 7in (12.7 x 17.8cm)
 or 6 x 8in (15.2 x 20.3cm) with
 suitable mount

Design size

3⅛ x 5¼in (7.9 x 13.3cm) at 14-count

Stitch count

44 x 73

Method

1   Find the centre of the fabric and begin stitching here, following the chart. Work the cross stitches over one block of fabric, referring to the instructions on page 14 if necessary.

2   Use two strands of thread for cross stitch as indicated in the key.

3   Once all the stitches have been completed press the fabric and mount within the chosen frame. Refer to page 18 if necessary for tips on framing.

Thread key

	DMC			DMC
■ Black	310		H Green	3347
✚ Pink Dark	347		✕ Green Deep	520
— Pink Pale	3713		& Green Pale	3348
E Pink	760		**French knots**	
S Pink Medium	3328		● Black	310

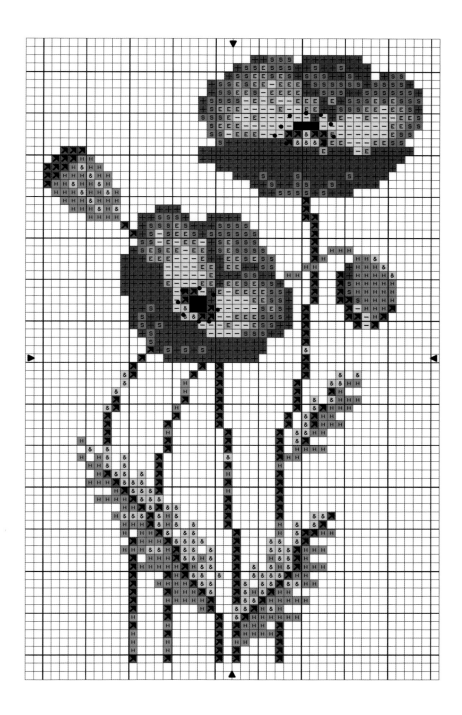

Poppy bookmark

Method

1 Find the centre of the fabric and begin stitching here, following the chart. Work the cross stitches over one block of fabric, referring to the instructions on page 14 if necessary.

2 Use two strands of thread for cross stitch, as indicated in the key.

3 Once all the stitches have been completed, press the fabric and mount within the bookmark following the same method for mounting three-fold cards (see page 18).

Materials

18-count white Aida, 3 x 8in (7.6 x 20.3cm) (Zweigart colour 100)
DMC stranded cotton, as listed in the key
Size 26 tapestry needle
Three-fold card bookmark blank

Design size

21 x 4¾in (53.3 x 12.1cm) at 18-count

Stitch count

18 x 85

Thread key

		DMC			DMC
■	Black	310	S	Pink Medium	3328
✚	Pink Dark	347	H	Green	3347
C	Pink Pale	3713	N	Green Grey	3052
E	Pink	760	G	Green Dark	3345

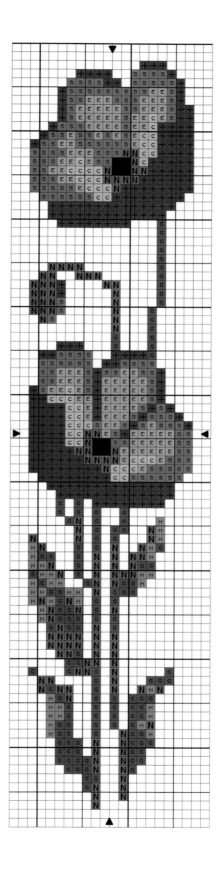

Poppy cards

These two cards are stitched using stitching paper which gives a lovely quality to them. The designs are finished off using beads and gold paper. They could be sent as cards to celebrate any occasion or simply used as notelets.

Method

1   Work both designs in the same way. Find the centre of the paper by measuring (do not fold), and begin stitching here, following the chart. Work the cross stitches over one block of fabric, referring to the instructions on page 14 if necessary.

2   Use two strands of thread for cross stitch as indicated in the key.

3   Once all the stitches have been completed, trim the paper to within two to three blocks of the finished design on all sides. Cut a piece of white paper the same size as the finished stitching and attach to the back (so that the gold paper doesn't show through).

4   Cut out a piece of gold paper slightly larger than the stitching paper and attach using either double-sided tape or a suitable glue. Attach the whole thing to the front of the card ensuring it is centred.

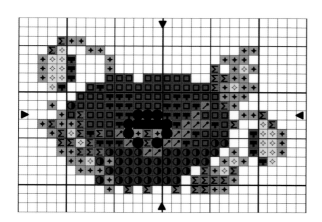

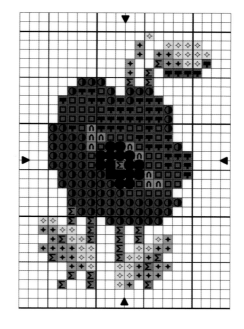

Materials (for both cards)

14-count white stitching paper, 3 x 4in
    (7.6 x 10.2cm)

DMC stranded cotton, as listed in the key

Size 26 tapestry needle

Two-fold card blank

Gold paper

Beads, as listed in the key

Design size

Landscape card: 1⅞ x 1¼in (4.7 x 3.2cm)
    at 14-count

Portrait card: 1¼ x 2in (3.2 x 5.1cm)
    at 14-count

Stitch count

Landscape card: 26 x 17

Portrait card: 18 x 28

Thread key	DMC		DMC
⋒ Peach	352	✦ Green	368
⬛ Red	666	Σ Olive Green	3363
⬛ Black	310	✧ Green Palest	772
◗ Red Medium	321	**Beads**	Mill Hill Seed
▣ Peach Dark	350	● Jet	00081

Clematis Patio Set

The clematis is another of my favourite flowers, representing mental beauty or intellectuality. It is wonderfully versatile in the garden, and is particularly adept at climbing up fences and walls. A genus of evergreen and deciduous plants, it is often referred to as 'old man's beard'. Clematis types can be classified according to their flowering time: early flowering, early large flowering and late large flowering.

The clematis flower is tastefully represented in the modern cushion design, and the chart for the coaster can easily be adapted to make a matching second cushion: use 14-count Aida and the same border as the original cushion stitched around; replace the centre panel of the cushion chart with the alternative chart and follow the instructions for making the cushion. The small picture could be made into a box lid, and the box used for keeping the coasters in. Stitch any of the flower motifs onto napkins or a table cloth, or even an Aida band to decorate a plant pot. For a more simple project, for a beginner, or if you don't have much spare time, the two cards can be completed in just a few hours, but are just as attractive.

Clematis cushion

Method

1 Find the centre of the fabric and begin stitching here, following the chart. Work the cross stitches over one block of fabric, referring to the instructions on page 14 if necessary.

2 Use two strands of thread for cross stitch and one for backstitch, as indicated in the key.

3 Once all the stitches have been completed, press the fabric.

Materials

14-count white Aida, 12 x 12in
  (30.5 x 30.5cm) (Zweigart colour 100)
Backing fabric, two pieces 11 x 18in
  (27.9 x 45.7cm)
Coloured fabric, 18 x 18in (45.7 x 45.7cm)
DMC stranded cotton, as listed in the key
Size 26 tapestry needle
Cushion (ready-made)

Design size

7¾ x 7¾in (19.7 x 19.7cm) at 14-count

Stitch count

108 x 108

Thread key	DMC		DMC
· Pink Pale	818	**Backstitch**	
+ Pink	3716	— Plum Light	3688
F Cerise Medium	3806	— Cerise Medium	3806
♥ Pink Medium Dark	603	— Violet Dark	552
V Violet	554	— Green Dark	986
Green Dark	986	— Plum	3803
G Green	989	**Beads**	Mill Hill Crayon
Pink Medium	605	• Yellow Green	02066
		• Green	02067

4 Trim the evenweave to 10 x 10in
(25.4 x 25.4cm), ensuring the design is centred.
Use small zig-zag stitches to stop the edges from
fraying. Stitch this centrally on the front panel of
the cushion cover.

5 Stitch the ribbon around the four edges of the
design to cover the edge.

6 Press and insert the cushion pad.

Clematis coaster

Method

1 Find the centre of the fabric and begin stitching here, following the chart. Work the cross stitches over one block of fabric, referring to the instructions on page 14 if necessary.

2 Use one strand of thread for cross stitch and one for backstitch, as indicated in the key.

3 Once all the stitches have been completed, press the fabric and mount within the coaster, following the manufacturer's instructions.

4 I would recommend that you use lightweight iron-on interfacing or Vilene to back the work. This will prevent it from fraying before cutting it out to fit the coaster.

Materials

22-count white Aida, 6 x 6in (15.2 x 15.2cm) (Zweigart colour 100)
DMC stranded cotton, as listed in the key
Size 26 tapestry needle
Square coaster
Iron-on interfacing or Vilene (optional)

Design size

3¼ x 3¼in (8.2 x 8.2cm) at 22-count

Stitch count

72 x 72

Thread key

		DMC			DMC
V	Violet	554	**Backstitch**		
◨	Green Dark	986	▬	Violet Dark	552
A	Green Pale Avocado	472	▬	Green Dark	986
G	Green	989	▬	Plum Light	3688
L	Green Pale	772	▬	Cerise Medium	3806
♥	Pink Medium Dark	603	▬	Plum	3803
■	Pink Medium	605			
·	Pink Pale	818	**French knots**		
✚	Pink	3716	●	Green Pale Avocado	472
F	Cerise Medium	3806			

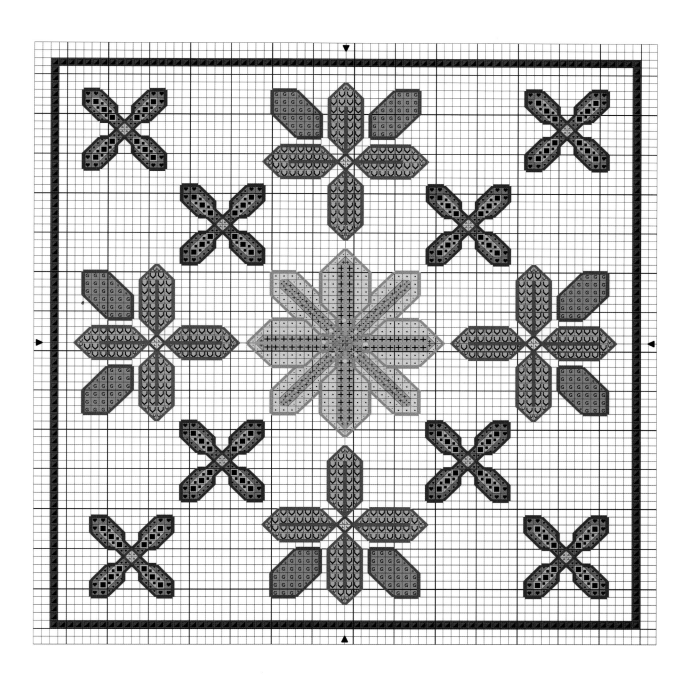

Clematis picture

Method

1 Find the centre of the fabric and start here following the chart. Work the cross stitches over one block of fabric, referring to the instructions on page 14 if necessary.

2 Use two strands of thread for cross stitch and one for backstitch, as indicated in the key.

3 Once all of the cross stitches have been completed, press the fabric and mount within the frame using the techniques on page 18 if necessary.

Materials

14-count white Aida, 8 x 8in (20.3 x 20.3cm)
    (Zweigart colour 100)
DMC stranded cotton, as listed in the key
Size 26 tapestry needle
Frame 8 x 8in (20.3 x 20.3cm) with suitable
    mount aperture of 4 x 4in (10.2 x 10.2cm)

Design size

3¾ x 3¾in (9.5 x 9.5cm) at 14-count

Stitch count

53 x 53

Thread key

		DMC			DMC
▲	Green	989	**Backstitch**		
◉	Green Dark	986	—	Green	989
P	Pink Medium Dark	603	—	Green Dark	986
M	Pink Medium	605	—	Pink Medium Dark	603
◥	Violet	554	—	Plum Light	3688
✚	Green Pale Avocado	472	—	Cerise Medium	3806
W	White	Blanc	—	Violet Dark	552
·	Pink Pale	818	**French knots**		
✚	Pink	3716	●	Green Pale Avocado	472
F	Cerise Medium	3806			
7	Green Pale	772			
6	Lavender	210			

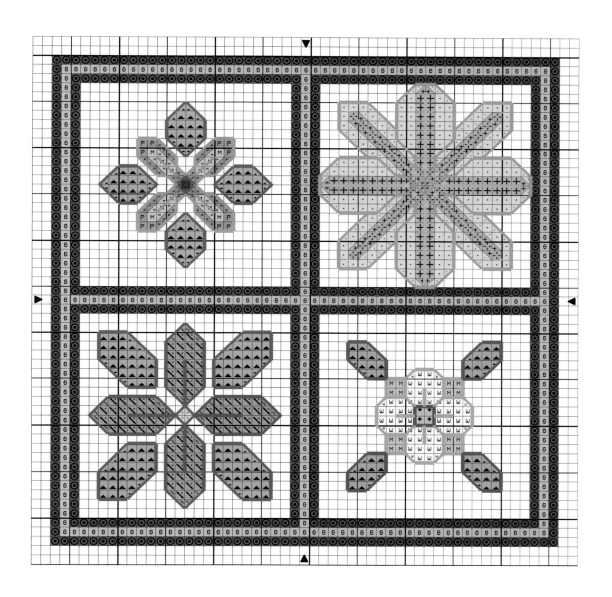

Clematis cards

Method

1   Work both cards in the same way. Find the centre of the fabric and start here following the chart. Work the cross stitches over one block of fabric, referring to the instructions on page 14 if necessary.

2   Use two strands of thread for cross stitch and one for backstitch, as indicated in the key.

3   Once all of the cross stitches have been completed, press the fabric and mount within the card using the techniques on page 18 if necessary.

Materials (for both cards)

14-count white Aida, 4 x 4in (10.2 x 10.2cm)
  (Zweigart colour 100)
DMC stranded cotton, as listed in the key
Size 26 tapestry needle
Three-fold card blank with square aperture
  2½ x 2½in (6.4 x 6.4cm)

Design size (for both cards)

1¾ x 1¾in (4.4 x 4.4cm) at 14-count

Stitch count (for both cards)

24 x 24

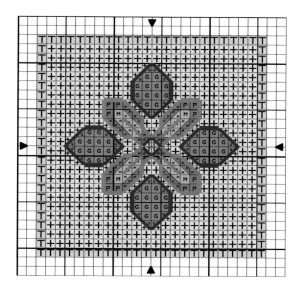

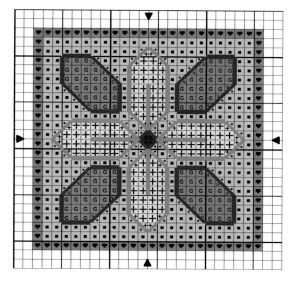

Pink card

Yellow card

Thread key

		DMC				DMC
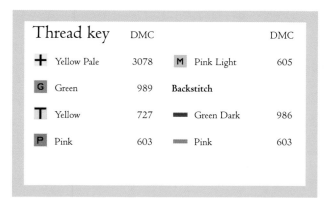 +	Yellow Pale	3078	M	Pink Light		605
G	Green	989		**Backstitch**		
T	Yellow	727			Green Dark	986
P	Pink	603			Pink	603

Thread key

		DMC				DMC
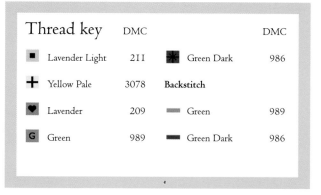 ■	Lavender Light	211	✱	Green Dark		986
+	Yellow Pale	3078		**Backstitch**		
♥	Lavender	209			Green	989
G	Green	989			Green Dark	986

Pictures

This collection of pictures is perfect for the more advanced stitcher, or even beginner seeking a challenging project. Ideal for brightening up that bare wall, or for giving as a gift with a personal touch.

The daffodil and tulip pictures are a good starting point, as they are small and fairly quick to stitch. The borders could be omitted and flowers then mounted within cards for any occasion. Once you have mastered these, you will find the iris picture a delight to stitch – it is deceptively simple, but the end result is very impressive.

Daffodils

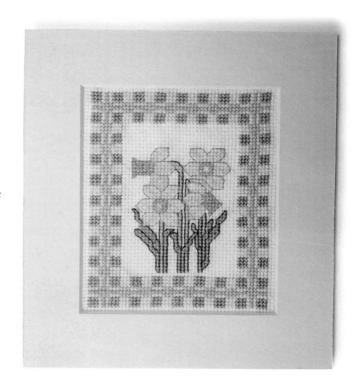

This bright pair of designs would liven up
any room. They contain cross stitch and backstitch
which helps to give the flowers the right shape. The
designs are small and fairly quick to stitch. The
borders could be omitted and the flowers then
mounted within cards which would be suitable for
any occasion. I have shown the tulip design
mounted in a three-fold card minus its border —
the daffodil design could be treated the same way.

Stitch both designs the same way.

Materials

14-count white Aida, 7 x 8in (17.8 x 20.3cm)
  (Zweigart colour 100)
DMC stranded cotton, as listed in the key
Size 26 tapestry needle
Suitable frame

Design size

3⅝ x 4½in (9.2 x 11.4cm) at 14-count

Stitch count

51 x 63

Thread key

	DMC			DMC
✚ Orange	740		Y Yellow	743
▨ Green	471	**Backstitch**		
· Green Pale	472	▬ Orange		740
♡ Yellow Pale	745	▬ Green Dark		3345
◄ Tangerine	741	▬ Yellow		743

Tulips

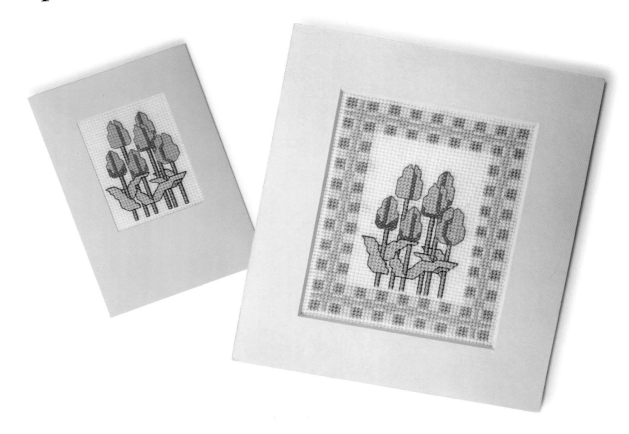

Materials

14-count white Aida, 7 x 8in (17.8 x 20.3cm)
  (Zweigart colour 100)
DMC stranded cotton, as listed in the key
Size 26 tapestry needle
Suitable frame and mount

Design size

3⅝ x 4½in (9.2 x 11.4cm) at 14-count

Stitch count

51 x 63

Method

1   Find the centre of the fabric and begin stitching here, following the chart. Work the cross stitches over one block of fabric, referring to the instructions on page 14 if necessary.

2   Use two strands of thread for cross stitch and one for backstitch, as indicated in the key.

3   Once all the stitches have been completed, press the fabric and mount within the chosen frame. Refer to page 18 if necessary for tips on framing.

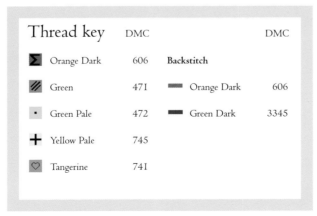

Thread key

		DMC			DMC
Σ	Orange Dark	606	**Backstitch**		
▨	Green	471	▬ Orange Dark	606	
·	Green Pale	472	▬ Green Dark	3345	
+	Yellow Pale	745			
♡	Tangerine	741			

Iris picture

The iris is one of my favourite flowers; I love their intense colour and shape. Their popularity can be seen in the still-life paintings of the Dutch masters, and more recently Vincent Van Gogh. Garden irises come in a broad spectrum of colours – in Greek, iris means 'rainbow' – though cut flower irises are commonly blue, white and yellow.

Here is a blue iris, which is deceptively simple to stitch. The design contains only whole cross stitch and backstitch. The backstitch is carefully placed to achieve a natural shape – watch how the design begins to come alive once you start adding the backstitch, though remember to add this once all the cross stitches have been completed.

Materials

14-count white Aida, 8 x 10in (20.3 x 25.4cm)
    (Zweigart colour 100)
DMC stranded cotton, as listed in the key
Size 26 tapestry needle
Frame with aperture 5 x 7in (12.7 x 17.8cm)
    or larger, with suitable mount

Design size

3⅞ x 5⅛in (9.8 x 13cm) at 14-count

Stitch count

54 x 72

Thread key	DMC		DMC
B Delft Blue	156	Green Forest Bright	907
Blue Violet	340	Yellow Pale	745
Blue Violet Medium	3746	**A** Yellow	726
Lavender Blue Dark	3838	Topaz	725
Blue Violet Light	341	**Backstitch**	
j Blue Violet Lightest	3747	Cornflower Blue	792
Green Dark	986	Green Dark	986
Green Forest Dark	905		

Method

1 Find the centre of the fabric and begin stitching here, following the chart. Work the cross stitches over one block of fabric, referring to the instructions on page 14 if necessary.

2 Use two strands of thread for cross stitch and one for backstitch, as indicated in the key.

3 Once all the stitches have been completed, press the fabric and mount within the chosen frame. Refer to page 18 if necessary for tips on framing.

Tulips picture

The name 'tulip' is inspired by its rounded form and comes from the Turkish for turban. In the Victorian language of flowers, red tulips are a declaration of love, but all colours except blue and true black are available.

This eye-catching vase of tulips has been designed with the more experienced stitcher in mind. The design contains half cross stitches and lots of backstitch. The tulips do look effective and are worth the extra effort required. I stitched the design using 28-count evenweave because half cross stitches are easier to make on this type of fabric rather than Aida. Also I think the design stands out from the fabric more than if stitched on Aida.

Materials

28-count white evenweave, 11 x 13in
  (27.9 x 33cm) (Zweigart colour 100)
DMC stranded cotton, as listed in the key
Size 26 tapestry needle
Frame with aperture 8 x 10in (20.3 x 25.4cm)
  and suitable mount

Design size

6⅜ x 7¾in (16.2 x 19.7cm) at 14-count

Stitch count

90 x 109

Thread key

		DMC				DMC
✔	Pink	3326		⦂	Winter White	3865
✚	Pink Medium	899		▬	Green Dark	319
ᴎ	Pink Light	963		◉	Pink Dark	3350
∧	Pink Palest	819		Σ	Lavender Dark	208
⬦	Pink Pale	818		**Half cross stitch**		
═	Lavender Medium	209		∴	Cream	712
U	Lavender Light	211		**Backstitch**		
⌐	Green Medium	368		▬	Green Dark	319
▦	Green Medium Dark	367		▬	Pink Dark	3350
⚒	Green Light	369		▬	Violet Deep	550
⋏	Lavender	210				

Method

1 Find the centre of the fabric and begin stitching here. Work the cross stitches over two threads of fabric, referring to the instructions on page 14 if necessary. Use two strands of thread for cross stitch and one for backstitch, as indicated in the key. Backstitch the tulips using 3350, the leaves using 319 and the vase using 550.

2 Once all the stitches are complete, press the fabric and mount within the chosen frame. Refer to page 18 for tips on framing.

Sunflower and poppy pictures

These two pictures are very simple but would give a lovely country effect to a room such as a kitchen or conservatory. Both designs are very easy to stitch and contain whole cross stitch, backstitch, and just a few colours, so are suitable for the beginner.

Method

1   Stitch both designs the same way. Find the centre of the fabric and begin stitching here, following the chart. Work the cross stitches over one block of fabric, referring to the instructions on page 14 if necessary.

2   Use two strands of thread for cross stitch and one for backstitch as indicated in the key.

3   After all the stitches have been completed press the fabric and mount within the chosen frame. Refer to page 18 if necessary for tips on framing.

Materials (for both pictures)

14-count white Aida, 6 x 8in (15.2 x 20.3cm) (Zweigart colour 100)
DMC stranded cotton, as listed in the key
Size 26 tapestry needle
Frame with aperture 3 x 5in (7.6 x 12.7cm)

Design size

2⅜ x 4⅜in (6.1 x 11.2cm) at 14-count

Stitch count

34 x 62

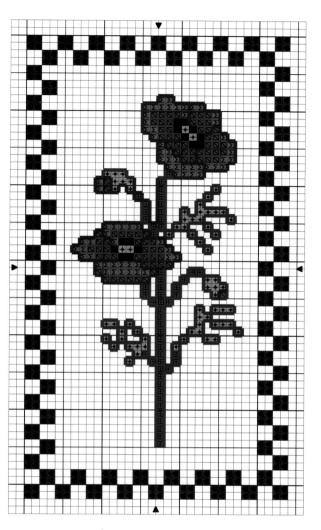

Sunflower picture

Poppy picture

Thread key	DMC			DMC
Green Medium	988		Brown Dark	801
Green	368		Brown Medium	435
Green Forest Medium	906		**Backstitch**	
Green Forest Dark	905		Green Forest Dark	905
Yellow	726		Brown Dark	801
Tangerine	742			

Thread key	DMC			DMC
Peach Dark	351		Black	310
Red	666		**Backstitch**	
Blue	798		Green Dark	319
Green	368		Grey	413
Green Medium	367			

Herb kitchen picture

Herbs have long been used for medicinal purposes, as well as to flavour food. Traditionally grown near the kitchen door, their delicious scent would waft into the house. Here I have chosen three popular herbs for this simple picture, which contains only whole cross stitch and backstitch and is suitable for the beginner. The herbs can be stitched individually and wrapped around herb jars, placed onto the front of a recipe book or used to liven up other kitchen items.

Method

1 Find the centre of the fabric and begin stitching here, following the chart. Work the cross stitches over one block of fabric referring to the instructions on page 14 if necessary.

2 Use two strands of thread for cross stitch and one for backstitch, as indicated in the key.

Backstitch the flower pots using 433, the flower detail using 335 and the text and leaves using 561.

3 After all the stitches have been completed press the fabric and mount within the chosen frame. Refer to page 18 if necessary for tips on framing.

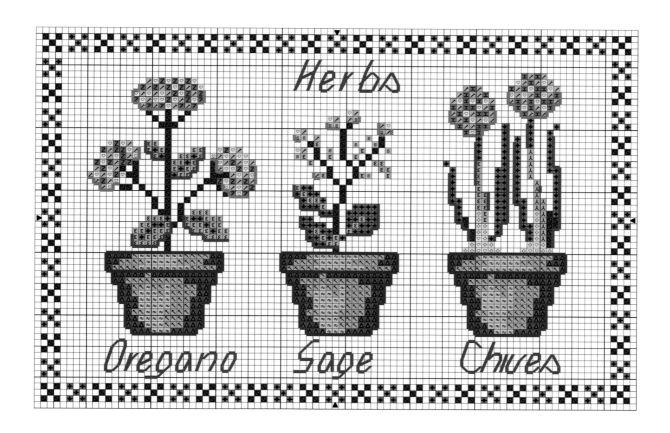

Materials

14-count white Aida, 10 x 8in (25.4 x 20.3cm)
  (Zweigart colour 100)
DMC stranded cotton, as listed in the key
Size 26 tapestry needle
Frame with aperture 8 x 6in (20.3 x 15.2cm)

Design size

6½ x 4¼in (16.5 x 10.8cm) at 14-count

Stitch count

91 x 59

Thread key

		DMC			DMC
6	Lavender Medium	210	♡	Pink Pale	819
◨	Jade Dark	561	➤	Pink	3326
⅄	Green Light	3817	⊞	Shell Pink	223
✦	Green Medium	163	Z	Pink Dark	335
↖	Terracotta Light	3856	**Backstitch**		
▲	Terracotta Dark	3776	—	Jade Dark	561
∼	Flesh	951	—	Brown	433
◇	Yellow	745	—	Pink Dark	335
Ɛ	Jade Light	563			

'Home sweet home' picture

Method

1   Find the centre of the fabric and begin stitching here, following the chart. Work the cross stitches over one block of fabric, referring to the instructions on page 14 if necessary.

2   Use two strands of thread for cross stitch and one for backstitch, as indicated in the key.

3   Once all the stitches have been completed, press the fabric and mount within the chosen frame. Refer to page 18 if necessary for tips on framing.

Materials

14-count white, Aida 8 x 6in (20.3 x 15.2cm)
  (Zweigart colour 100)
DMC stranded cotton, as listed in the key
Size 26 tapestry needle
Frame with aperture 5 x 3in (12.7 x 7.6cm)

Design size

4½ x 2½in (11.4 x 6.4cm) at 14-count

Stitch count

63 x 35

Thread key

		DMC			DMC
L	Pink	3326	♡	White	Blanc
	Lavender Light	211	1	Ecru	Ecrut
○	Blue Violet	340	ℓ	Antique Gold	3822
=	Violet	554	▦	Brown	612
	Green	3816	**Backstitch**		
	Green Dark	367	▬	Brown Dark	610
V	Green Light	368	**French knots**		
⋏	Gold	676	●	Brown Dark	610

Contemporary and Traditional Cards

The four contemporary cards have a modern theme and are suitable for any occasion. You could stitch and mount them in square coasters if you prefer, and the tiny flowers could be stitched as matching gift tags, too. As each design has only a few colours, you could experiment and change them to achieve different effects.

The pair of traditional cards would be well-received as a gift. Framed in their card mount after the event, they would be a lasting reminded of the occasion. Stitched using 14-count Aida, both are simple and quick to make.

Purple and pink cards

Materials for all four cards

14-count white Aida, 6 x 6in (15.2 x 15.2cm)
  (Zweigart colour 100)
DMC stranded cotton, as listed in the key
Size 26 tapestry needle
Three-fold card blank with aperture 3 x 3in
  (7.6 x 7.6cm)

Design size

2¾ x 2¾in (7 x 7cm) at 14-count

Stitch count

Pink and purple cards: 40 x 40
Yellow and blue cards: 42 x 42

Thread key		DMC
⊼	Violet	153
=	Blue Violet	340
6	Lavender	210
C	Green	955
Backstitch		
—	Green	955

Thread key		DMC
f	Pink Pale	963
+	Pink Medium	604
N	Pink Dark	602
C	Green	955
Backstitch		
—	Green	955

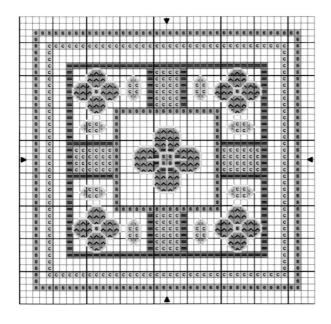

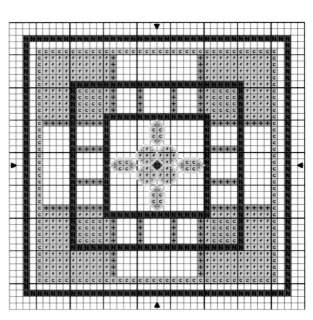

Yellow and blue cards

Stitch all four cards in the same way.

Method

1   Find the centre of the fabric and begin stitching here, following the chart. Work the cross stitches over one block of fabric, referring to the instructions on page 14 if necessary.

2   Use two strands of thread for cross stitch and one for backstitch, as indicated in the key.

3   Once all the stitches have been completed, press the fabric and mount within the card. Refer to page 18 if necessary.

Thread key	DMC
∧ Yellow Pale	3078
A Yellow	726
C Green	955
Backstitch	
— Green	955

Thread key	DMC
◇ Blue Pale	3761
∧ Yellow Pale	3078
N Blue Medium	807
C Green	955
Backstitch	
— Green	955

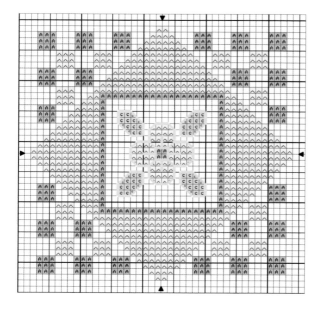

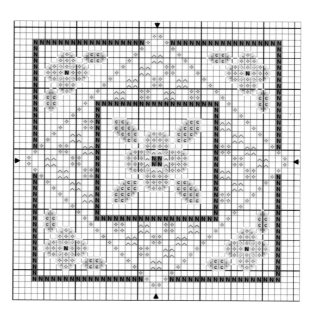

Delphinium card

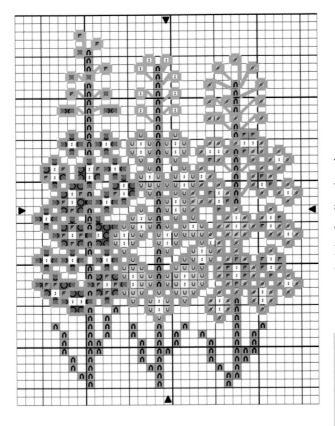

The name delphinium comes from the Latin word 'delphis', meaning dolphin – due to the shape of the buds. Originating in China, the delphinium is available mainly in shades of blue, purple and white, but salmon and yellow forms can also be found.

Materials

14-count white Aida, 5 x 5in (12.7 x 12.7cm) (Zweigart colour 100)
DMC stranded cotton, as listed in the key
Size 26 tapestry needle
Three-fold card blank with circular aperture

Design size

2¼ x 3⅛in (5.7 x 8.6cm) at 14-count

Stitch count

31 x 43

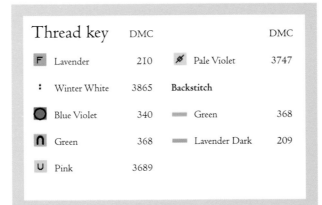

Thread key	DMC		DMC
F Lavender	210	∅ Pale Violet	3747
: Winter White	3865	**Backstitch**	
◯ Blue Violet	340	— Green	368
∩ Green	368	— Lavender Dark	209
U Pink	3689		

Fuchsia card

Flowering between early summer and autumn, the fuchsia has bell-shaped flowers that are often bi-coloured. Trailing varieties are popular for hanging baskets, a common sight in gardens, though there are also shrub and tree varieties.

Materials

14-count white Aida, 5 x 5in (12.7 x 12.7cm)
    (Zweigart colour 100)
DMC stranded cotton, as listed in the key
Size 26 tapestry needle
Three-fold card blank with circular aperture

Design size

2¼ x 2¾in (5.7 x 7cm) at 14-count

Stitch count

31 x 39

Method

1   Find the centre of the fabric and begin stitching here, following the chart. Work the cross stitches over one block of fabric, referring to page 14if necessary.

2   Use two strands of thread for cross stitch and one for backstitch as indicated in the key.

3   Once all the stitches have been completed, press the fabric and mount in the card, referring to page 18 if necessary.

Thread key

		DMC			DMC
♡	Pink Palest	819	**Backstitch**		
H	Green Light	369	▬	Pink Deep	3328
∩	Green	368	▬	Green Dark	367
✚	Pink	760	**French knots**		
◣	Pink Deep	3328	●	Pink Deep	3328
f	Pink Pale	963			

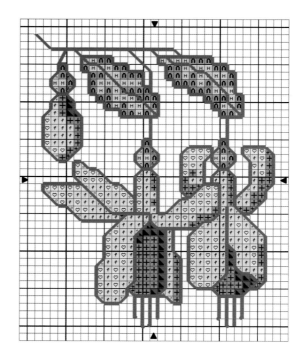

Floral Motifs and Gifts

Here is a selection of small flower motifs, I have illustrated a few of them stitched up and mounted. All are simple to make and could be used on many different items, so don't feel limited by my suggestions. For example, you could stitch the sunflower as a bookmark and attach the plant-pot button at the bottom of the stem, or you could stitch them on different coloured fabrics. Remember that the instructions for finding the finished size are on pages 11–12. You can adjust the finished size by choosing a higher- or lower-count fabric.

Floral motifs

Thread key

		DMC			DMC			DMC			DMC
c	Pink Pale	818		Topaz	725		Violet Dark	550	—	Violet Dark	550
	Pink Medium	3326		Yellow Pale	744		Pink Dark	961	—	Raspberry	347
n	Pink Deep	899		Tangerine	741	F	Pink	3689	—	Pink Dark	961
j	Lavender Light	211	•	White	Blanc		Blue Violet Dark	3746	—	Blue Violet Dark	3746
6	Lavender	210		Green Dark	319	2	Yellow Green Pale	3348	**French Knots**		
	Lavender Dark	208		Green Medium Light	320	•	Yellow Green Medium	472		Topaz	725
Σ	Green	987		Raspberry	347	**Backstitch**				Tangerine	742
	Green Medium Dark	986		Green Medium	367	—	Pink Deep	899		Green Dark	319
	Beige Dark	613		Green Light	368	—	Beige Very Dark	612		Violet Dark	550
	Beige Very Dark	612	H	Green Lightest	369	—	Green Dark	319			

Organza bag

Materials

'White Heart' appliqué patch (available from DMC)

DMC stranded cotton, as listed in the key

Size 26 tapestry needle

Two pieces of organza fabric, 6 x 8in (15.2 x 20.3cm)

Decorative cord, 12in (30.5cm) long

Pot pourri

Design size

1¼ x ⅞in (3.2 x 2.2cm) at 14-count

Stitch count

17 x 12

Method

1   Find the centre of the fabric and begin stitching here, following the chart. Work the cross stitches over one block of fabric, referring to the instructions on page 14 if necessary.

2   Use two strands of thread for cross stitch and one for backstitch, as indicated in the key.

3   Once all the stitches have been completed, press the patch.

4   With the right sides together, stitch the two pieces of organza fabric along the sides and bottom.

5   Sew a small hem along the top all the way around. Turn the bag the right way around and stitch the lace along the top.

6   Fill the bag with dried lavender or pot pourri and tie a length of cord around the top to fasten. Stitch the patch to the front of the organza bag.

Diary and rosebud card

Method for diary

1 Find the centre of the fabric and begin stitching the bottom line of the flower chart here. Work the cross stitches over two threads of fabric, referring to the instructions on page 14 if necessary. Use two strands of thread for cross stitch and one for backstitch, as indicated in the key.

2 After all the stitching has been completed press the fabric before attaching the button below the motif using brown thread.

3 Trim the patch and, using suitable glue, attach to the front of the diary. You may find backing the patch with iron-on interfacing or Vilene before attaching will help prevent the fabric fraying.

Method for card

1 Find the centre of the fabric and begin stitching here, following the chart. Work the cross stitches over one block of fabric, referring to the instructions on page 14 if necessary.

2 Use two strands of thread for cross stitch and one for backstitch, as indicated in the key.

3 After the stitches are complete, press the fabric and mount in the card, referring to page 18.

Materials for diary

28-count white evenweave, 4 x 5in (10.2 x 12.7cm)
DMC stranded cotton, as listed in the key
Size 26 tapestry needle
Suitable diary or notebook
Plant-pot talisman buttons
Iron-on interfacing or Vilene (optional)

Design size

1 x 1in (2.5 x 2.5cm) at 14-count

Stitch count

18 x 20

Materials for card

14-count white Aida, 5 x 6in (12.7 x 15.2cm)
DMC stranded cotton, as listed in the key
Size 26 tapestry needle
Three-fold card blank with oval aperture

Design size

1½ x 2¼in (3.8 x 5.7cm) at 14-count

Stitch count

23 x 31

Suppliers and Sources of Information

Below is a list of suppliers who have kindly provided the materials used in the stitching and mounting of the designs in this book, and a selection of other sources who can supply mail-order products for your own cross-stitch designs.

UK

DMC Creative World Ltd
Pullman Road
Wigson, Leicester
LE18 2DY, UK
Tel: + 44 (0) 1162 811040
Website: www.dmc.com
Zweigart fabrics, DMC threads, beads and accessories.

Framecraft
Lichfield Road
Brownhills
Walsall
West Midlands WS8 6LH, UK
Tel: + 44 (0) 1543 360842
Website: www.Framecraft.com
Coasters, wooden boxes, ceramic bowls, charms and a wide range of plastic items and Mill Hill beads.

Craft Creations
Ingersall House
Delamare Road
Cheshunt, Hertfordshire
EN8 9HD, UK
Tel: + 44 (0) 1992 781900
Website: www.craftcreations.com
Three-fold cards and other craft items.

Fulford Software Solutions
93 Penrhyn Crescent
Chilwell, Nottingham
NG9 5PA, UK
Tel: + 44 (0) 1159 678761
Email: sales@easycross.co.uk
Cross-stitch computer software.

Talisman Buttons
29 Coutts Avenue
Shorne, Gravesend
Kent DA12 3HJ
Tel: + 44 (0) 1474 822960
Novelty buttons.

Oliver Twists
22 Phoenix Road
Crowther, Washington
Tyne and Wear
NE38 0A, UK
Tel: + 44 (0) 191 416 6016
Email: jean@olivertwists.freeserve.co.uk
Variegated and multi-coloured threads.

Coates Crafts
PO Box 22
Lingfield House
Lingfield Point
McMullen Road
Darlington, Co. Durham
DL1 1YQ, UK
Tel: + 44 (0) 1325 394237
Website: www.coatscrafts.co.uk
Stranded cotton, variegated threads and stitching items.

Debbie Cripps
8 Christchurch Street West
Frome, Somerset
BA11 1EQ, UK
Tel: + 44 (0) 1373 454448
Website: www.debbiecripps.co.uk
Doilies, novelty buttons, charms and other stitching items.

HobbyCraft Group Ltd
7 Enterprise Way, Aviation Park
Bournemouth International Airport
Christchurch, Dorset
BH23 6HG, UK
Tel: + 44 (0) 1202 596100
Website: www. hobbycraft.co.uk
Large range of art and craft materials.

Card Art
14 Kensington Industrial Park
Hall Street, Southport, Merseyside
PR9 0NY, UK
Tel: + 44 (0) 1704 536040
Email: enq@cardart.co.uk
Extensive selection of paper, cards and craft items.

The Thread Mill
4 Church Street, Swinton
Mexborough, South Yorkshire
S64 8QA, UK
Tel: + 44 (0) 1709 571684
Website: www.threadmill.co.uk
Wide range of stitching materials.

Fabric Flair
Warminster, Wiltshire
BA12 0BG, UK
Tel: + 44 (0) 1985 846400
Website: www.fabricflair.com
Wide range of fabrics for cross stitch.

North America

Charles Craft
PO Box 1049
Laurinburg
NC 28352, USA
Tel: (910) 844 3521
Fax: (910) 844 9846
Email: email@charlescraft.com
Fine line of cross-stitch fabric and pre-finished accessories.

Crafter's Pride
PO Box 1105
Laurinburg
NC 28353, USA
Tel: (910) 277 7441
Fax: (910) 277 837
Email: email@craftersprice.com
Top quality cross-stitch pre-finished accessories and designs.

About the Author

Joanne Sanderson worked for a number of years as a qualified Registered General Nurse. Her passion for cross stitch was inspired when asked by a friend to produce a design for her. A few months later, she entered and won a national competition to design a greetings card in cross stitch, which was great inspiration. She decided to give up nursing and build on her passion for cross stitch by designing patterns full time. It was a very successful decision; her designs regularly feature in many popular cross-stitch magazines, and she has recently been commissioned by DMC to design cross-stitch kits. In her spare time, Joanne's great passions are art, nature and gardening. She lives with her husband, daughter and two cats in South Yorkshire, England.

This is her second book for GMC Publications, and she is currently working on her third book and further kit designs for DMC.

Index

Page numbers in **bold** refer to photographs and illustrations